T0329560

Single Stock Futures

WILEY TRADING SERIES

SINGLE STOCK FUTURES
A TRADER'S GUIDE

Patrick L. Young and Charles Sidey

John Wiley & Sons, Ltd

Published 2003   John Wiley & Sons Ltd, The Atrium, Southern Gate, Chichester, West Sussex PO19 8SQ, England

Telephone   (+44) 1243 779777

Email (for orders and customer service enquiries): cs-books@wiley.co.uk
Visit our Home Page on www.wileyeurope.com or www.wiley.com

Other Wiley Editorial Offices

John Wiley & Sons, Inc., 111 River Street, Hoboken, NJ 07030, USA

Jossey-Bass, 989 Market Street, San Francisco, CA 94103-1741, USA

Wiley-VCH Verlag GmbH, Boschstr. 12, D-69469 Weinheim, Germany

John Wiley & Sons Australia Ltd, 33 Park Road, Milton, Queensland 4064, Australia

John Wiley & Sons (Asia) Pte Ltd, 2 Clementi Loop #02-01, Jin Xing Distripark, Singapore 129809

John Wiley & Sons Canada Ltd, 22 Worcester Road, Etobicoke, Ontario, Canada M9W 1L1

Wiley also publishes its books in a variety of electronic formats. Some content that appears in print may not be available in electronic books.

Library of Congress Cataloging-in-Publication Data

Young, Patrick L.
   Single stock futures : a traders guide / Patrick Young and Charles Sidey.
      p. cm.—(Wiley trading series)
   Includes bibliographical references and index.
   ISBN 0-470-85315-8 (alk. paper)
   1. Single stock futures. 2. Futures. I. Sidey, Charles. II. Title. III. Series.
HG6041.Y68 2003
332.63′228—dc21   2003045068

British Library Cataloguing in Publication Data

A catalogue record for this book is available from the British Library

ISBN 0-470-85315-8

Project management by Originator, Gt Yarmouth, Norfolk (typeset in 10/12pt Times)

Contents

To Iain Cain for being a great friend, the finest host on the Côte d'Azur and simply the best impromptu singer with which any late night soirée can be blessed!

To Gaby for providing unstinting support and encouragement at all time, which I hope I can return in the future.

Foreword

It all started at Wiltons. A lot of things to do. Somewhere between the quail eggs and the bread pudding our conversation turned to the challenge that was facing my friend.

It was 1997 and Sir Brian Williamson had just agreed to become Chairman of Liffe—the embattled derivatives exchange that was fighting for survival. Its demise would be a significant chink in London's armor and threaten the city's preeminence as a financial center. The first step was clear: close the floor and migrate all trading to an electronic platform. Easily said, but never before successfully accomplished on this scale. The second step was equally challenging. Invent a product complex that had the potential to be as significant as the interest rate complex.

As a student of markets the path was obvious. Equity derivatives had a long history. Futures and options on single stocks had been traded in Amsterdam in the 17th century. Their natural evolution demonstrated their importance as a risk-shifting mechanism. For a variety of institutional and legal reasons they were dormant for centuries. Modern equity derivatives began in 1973 at the Chicago Board Options Exchange and had been successfully imitated worldwide. This was followed by the invention of stock index futures at the Kansas City Board of Trade. These were successfully innovated at the Chicago Mercantile Exchange and ultimately imitated worldwide. The missing piece of the puzzle was a futures market on single stocks. I had unsuccessfully tried to fill this gap in 1982 at the Chicago Board of Trade with the design of narrowly-based indices, which in some industries were surrogates for single stocks. This led to the Shad–Johnson accord between the SEC[1] and CFTC,[2] which banned narrowly-based indices. The legal ban on single stock futures and surrogates still left the complex incomplete.

While the elimination of the ban in the United States seemed daunting the prospects in London seemed better, particularly if it was championed by the right individual. It required the vision of a divergent or outsider mentality coupled with competencies of a convergent or insider mentality. Sir Brian had these qualities. Ultimately the stamp tax on futures disappeared and the Bank of England and the Securities and Futures Authority recognized the rationality of the concept. The timing was also right. Debt was a 1980s commodity and equity a 1990s commodity. The U.S. financial sector provided the paradigm. In 1990, there was $2 trillion in the form of Federal debt in the U.S. Ten years later that figure had risen to $3 trillion, while during the same period the size of the U.S. equity market rose from $3 to $14 trillion. Europe was having a similar transformation.

By the time the armagnac and cigars arrived the path seemed clear. One last question remained. How would this resonate in the United States? Liffe would list both U.S. and European stocks. This would inevitably result in political pressures to lift the U.S. ban. We thought that would ultimately broaden the interest in the markets and become a catalyst for a self-fulfilling prophecy. Several years later LIFFE launched Universal Stock Futures. It was successfully imitated in continental Europe. The ban in the United States was lifted and OneChicago and NQLX[3] launched single stock futures in N.Y. and Chicago in 2002. Liffe had a record volume that very same year. A lot had happened in a short five years.

It was a wonderful dinner with a dear friend.

Richard Sandor
Chicago, January, 2003

---

[1] SEC—Securities & Exchange Commission, the US regulator for equity trading.
[2] CFTC—Commodities Futures Trading Commission, the US commodities and futures regulator.
[3] NQLX—originally standing for NASDAQ LIFFE markets, NASDAQ withdrew in mid-2003, leaving Euronext LIFFE in sole control. NQLX along with OneChicago are the two principal US single stock futures exchanges.

Acknowledgements

To list everybody who has provided input on *Single Stock Futures: A Trader's Guide* is a tricky issue but as ever we'll try ... on the premise that all omissions are ours and we sincerely appreciate everybody who has helped us to create this tome: James Barr, Max Butti, Caterina Caramaschi, Caroline Denton, James Dunseath, John Foyle, Hugh Freedburg, Juliette Proudlove, Simon Raybould, Sir Brian Williamson, Denise and Geoff at Euronext LIFFE reception/switchboard (who always thought we wouldn't mention them—as if!!!), Nick Carew Hunt, Sonny Schneider, Jonathan Seymour, Luis Velasco, David Lascelles at CSFI whose report "The Ultimate Derivative" we can wholeheartedly recommend, Richard Sandor, NQLX: Bob Fitzsimmons, OneChicago: Bob Paul. Also to Mike Charlton, Steve Smith, Carlo Antonioli, Paul Meier, Carol Gregoir, Paul-André Jacot, and Joe Murphy.

Our fellow directors at erivatives Brendan Bradley and Giuliano Gregorio also deserve our thanks for their assistance, as do Seana Lanigan and Hilary Redmond.

On the social front, there are various folks who must be thanked for keeping Patrick "sane" during the trials and tribulations of book-writing: Iain Cain (for everything from drinks and dinner to a variety of splendid experiences on the Elvis and Sinatra front!), Lucrecia Vogogna for her generous hospitality just when deadlines were looming, Charlie Sidey and Gaby Leiders always keep a wonderfully hospitable household, while Patrick and Monique Birley have now extended their hospitality to a new continent somewhat distant from their native South Africa. In Monaco, a night out is simply never the same without the company of various, really fun folk, among whom I would like to thank for their constant encouragement: Chimese, Emma Jane, Marie Claire, Liza, Manfred, Heidi, Seonaid, and "tric o trac" Paolone. Thanks too to Clara and Paolo for their ongoing words of encouragement and general excitement as this book reached its gestation.

Elsewhere, my thanks also go to my mother Joan who, despite having read my previous tomes, is still impressed that I am a published author, while various folk deserve a mention if only for being helpful to what can often be a self-absorbed author, in this respect my heartfelt thanks go to Diane, Ina, Laura, and Lutz.

While not so glamorous, the leafy wilderness of Petts Wood on the borders of Kent and South-East London also provides a wealth of people (and dogs) who provide a reality and sanity that is truly warming. Peter and Barbera Woods for their constant, indispensable, neighbourly support and encouragement. Wilfried Schnedler, Nick Fuller, Bea Groeger, and Gaby Leiders for allowing me to invade "the bunker" and use their facilities over many hours.

Allistair and Vivienne and Nathan Woods, Lesley Boxall, Tony Marshall, Clive Roberts, Mike Stiller, John, Joanne, Grace and Molly Hopkins, Kevin Mitchell, Lisa Boxall, Graham Hughes, Lance Roberts, Tim Ockenden and Grahem Weaver, who have all given their support unselfishly. John Spencer and all the dogs and their owners who walk in Petts Wood, who listen patiently, offer encouragement at each pace, and manage to change the subject with such subtlety. My own dog Bella who now knows more about Single Stock Futures than I do! I must thank all the staff at the Homefield Nursing Home in Bickley whose dedication and excellent care of my mother Ana Maria has allowed me to concentrate more fully on the production of this book. My brothers Peter and Joseph and Mairi and Bethany who have lightened the burden along the way.

To everybody who has contributed to this tome, even indirectly, our grateful thanks.

Charlie Sidey
Patrick L. Young
London and Monaco, December, 2002

Introduction: Another New Product, Another Revolution

Universal Stock Futures represent a revolution in global equity trading. They will be easy, cheap and efficient to trade.

Sir Brian Williamson, Executive Chairman, LIFFE, announcing the launch of the world's first international stock futures, September 20, 2000

Single Stock Futures (SSFs) represent the most exciting new product launch within the equity derivatives arena since the derivatives bandwagon began exploding in the post-Bretton Woods era of financial deregulation. Their development has been hampered by regulatory issues in the USA, but the launch of NASDAQ LIFFE, and OneChicago in November 2002 brought SSFs to the world's largest capital market for the first time.

The history of SSFs, as we will outline in Chapter 1, has been a somewhat tortured one, with historical precedents evident in 17th century Amsterdam, although the modern products initially have had a fairly chequered history during the past decade. Nevertheless, nobody can underestimate the sensational potential for SSFs (which in any case have been available both Over The Counter [OTC] and synthetically through options exchanges for some 20 years). Throughout history, the introduction of futures products have enhanced liquidity and trading opportunities in the cash market as well as creating a significant new dimension for traders, hedgers, and risk-managers seeking to improve their returns or sleep easier at night. In an increasingly digital financial market environment, SSFs are a key element of the development of equity derivative products.

The origins of modern SSFs begin in Asia, as we will discuss in Chapter 2. However, within Europe and the USA, their introduction (well, one could argue it was their "reintroduction" given their invention in Amsterdam centuries ago) was championed first by the LIFFE exchange in London (although the MEFF in Spain neatly managed to launch just ahead of the London market in early January 2001) and subsequently in North America by the Bourse de Montreal later that month (Montreal launched in January 2001 also). Having first championed SSFs as early as July 1997 in Appliederivatives (http://www.appliederivatives.com) in an article entitled "The Next Frontier", one of the authors of this book Patrick L. Young was a keen observer of the development of SSFs; indeed, in the late 1990s they were largely off the agenda in the US marketplace. However, the ongoing bull market of the late 1990s helped fuel interest in equity derivatives products, while LIFFE's announcement of their intention to be the first major international exchange to launch SSFs in 2001 was a pivotal moment in the development of the product. Patrick L. Young was actively involved in the launch of LIFFE's Universal Stock Futures product and subsequently enjoyed working with Bourse de Montreal on their marketplace as well. Doctor Richard Sandor, rightly acclaimed as the "father of financial futures", was a pivotal figure in the introduction of SSFs on LIFFE and in the USA, while it was Sir Brian Williamson's legendary foresight that helped steer the launch of the product on LIFFE and indeed the creation of the groundbreaking LIFFE/NASDAQ venture in the USA—of which more later.

As Doctor Richard Sandor has frequently noted[4] the 1990s marked a shift in capital from a debt-oriented to an equity-oriented society. The US debt remained essentially stable at about $3 billion. However, during the same period, the equity market increased to almost $14 billion. Therefore, with the vast increase in global equity, it was entirely appropriate that this paradigm shift in investment should be accompanied by a similar move toward increased quantities of equity derivative products, and indeed volumes in options and stock index futures have been exploding during the past 10 years and more. The SSF revolution is at its very core fuelled by an increasing demand for all forms of equity products.

Despite the bear market in equities during the early part of the 21st century, Doctor Sandor's thesis remains highly pertinent. The aging of the world's population has led to a greater pressure on pensions and therefore created a requirement to push financial assets to a greater degree to meet future liabilities. Even if the stock market goes through a decade of relative underperformance, the need for increasing equity products is not going to abate. SSFs have

---

[4] Quoted in *Capital Market Revolution, the Winners, the Losers and the Future of Finance*, Texere Publishing, 2003, and much discussed on the LIFFE US Single Stock Futures (USF) roadshows 2001.

a multiplicity of advantages for many types of trader and investor, being a cheap, easy-to-understand, and highly efficient use of capital to enhance investor opportunities. The ongoing impact of the SSF revolution will lead to greater underlying liquidity in the cash market as market-makers are able to make better prices based upon the opportunity to use another instrument (in addition to options, warrants et al.) to hedge their stock positions. Indeed, in many respects single stock futures may provide an opportunity to help tighten bid/offer spreads in the cash equity market to a greater degree than even the much vaunted move to decimalization of US stock prices introduced during 2001.

The dynamics of futures trading are similar, but subtly different to those of the equity exchanges. In this book, we aim to provide insights into the trading of these new products that will assist both the retail and the professional trader in understanding the risks and opportunities behind SSFs. Overall, the trading universe has been significantly enhanced by the arrival of SSFs and we hope that from this book you will understand just how you can benefit from this revolution.

This book is an entirely joint collaboration by Charles Sidey and Patrick L. Young. We have been colleagues and friends for some 15 years, first at Tullett and Tokyo Futures in the late 1980s and early 1990s and then through various other ventures, including the online publishing company "erivatives.com" where we both serve as directors. We welcome any feedback on this book, and we hope you will enjoy and profit from reading it.

Good trading!

Charles Sidey
Patrick L. Young
London, November, 2002

Prologue: The Next Frontier[5]

Amid all the delicious discussion about innovation within this business, the last few years have witnessed a substantial paradigm shift in favour of ever more exotic and esoteric instruments. Having said that, developments such as Credit derivatives are very exciting—these splendid new methods for reducing risk will undoubtedly enjoy considerable growth in the forthcoming years. Other new products of a similar nature will doubtless also emerge. However, among the vast numbers of derivatives that are now available, one area looks significantly under-represented. What's more, it's a plain vanilla product and ought to be the perfect listing fodder for any of the multiplicity of exchanges currently competing so strongly for a volume edge in an increasingly competitive business.

In the 1970s and 1980s, it was first currency futures and then Treasury Bond futures that revolutionized trading. However, while the Value Line future on the Kansas City Board of Trade led to the Chicago Board of Trade (CBOT) Major Market Index and the CME S&P500 futures indices, this has failed to trickle through to individual stock-trading. True, one could argue that bond futures—due to the lists of deliverable bonds—are themselves a form of index, as they represent a series of securities. However, these bonds are different securities only in so far as their yields, which are but functions of the dynamics of interest rate markets. The issuer of a Treasury Bond is invariably the same for each security—although European Monetary Union (EMU) may result in the first major divergence from this trend.

---

[5] This article was first published by Patrick L. Young in http://www.appliederivatives. com during July 1997, when Single Stock Futures (SSFs) were essentially off the agenda of the major exchanges. Nowadays, of course, most exchanges have talked of little else in recent months ... Oh, and at the time this article provoked wails of protest from a number of readers who reckoned there was simply no good reason to see why SSFs ought to be listed.

It is, therefore, difficult to understand why there has not been a greater move toward listing futures on individual equities. True, the initial experiments in such contracts have hardly been overwhelmingly successful. They have, however, been launched in rather far-flung parts and generally on second-tier exchanges. Moreover, they have tended to be in competition with existing options contracts listed on rival stock exchanges.

In Chicago, the CBOT and CME have shown no great disposition to list individual stock futures, perhaps as a result of the CBOE maintaining an overwhelming position in individual equity options. Quite why the latter cannot see the advantages of listing futures to complement their current products rather escapes me. There are regulatory considerations in the Shad–Johnson Accord (see p. 4), but a satisfactory framework could surely be found if there was a serious desire to do so.

In London, LIFFE has been recalcitrant about listing individual stock futures. Presumably, this is at least in part due to the fact that equity options have continued to post disappointing volumes, relative to the size and importance of the London equity markets. In Paris, rivalry between the MONEP equity options market and MATIF futures exchange may well be counterproductive to the development of futures. The increasing fixation with EMU is further likely to slow down the process of listing such products in Europe.

Yet the arguments for stock futures are considerable—and overwhelmingly favourable to the development of not only the derivatives markets but continued growth in the cash markets as well. Unfortunately, many major stockbrokers appear to lack the vision that stock futures would actually improve their bottom line, rather than harming the precious commissions of their salespeople.

Take the process of market-making for instance. True, many stock markets work on an order-driven basis. Nevertheless, here too, significant advantages could be enjoyed. For a start, primary dealers/market-makers would have the opportunity to not only trade the underlying cash but the futures—and quite probably options—too. This way, they could limit their risks much more efficiently. Indeed, increasing liquidity in the futures contract would permit the narrowing of spreads among the stock market-makers. And let's face it, the spreads in stock markets in many parts of the world could do with a bit of narrowing in order to encourage greater interest from short-term players. Would anybody care to argue that narrower bid–ask spreads discourage more business?

So, individual stock futures would reduce the bid–offer spread and therefore increase volume in all markets. Furthermore, this added liquidity is likely to come not merely from existing traders, it would doubtless also arise from new sources. For one thing, market-makers in options and derivatives products would be interested in the increasing sophistication of trading stocks. And the judicious use of derivative products would reduce the capital cost of primary dealing. Again, this would enhance liquidity and lead to a more genuine market, at least in the leading stocks.

For example, as things currently stand, it would be no exaggeration to state that genuine liquidity only extends through perhaps the largest third of the London FTSE 100 Index. With stock futures, there is no reason to believe that such markets could not enhance liquidity throughout the entire top 100 equities—and perform a similar function on the rest of the world's major bourses. And, of course, the advantage in even the most liquid stocks would be considerable.

Other sources of new investment in the equities market would likely include many derivatives-based proprietary traders, such as this correspondent. True, I might only be a tick on the back of a great rhinoceros such as the Quantum Fund. But at the moment I don't go near individual stocks, as it is simply too capital-intensive. Show me a liquid stock future, however, and I'm not just going to be interested in outrights, but in a good many intriguing cash/futures/ options strategies as well.

Of course, when it comes to short-selling, current stock market regulations worldwide tend to be particularly onerous—and rather disadvantageous to the prospective short-seller. But once we get into futures land, all these drawbacks are effortlessly waved away. True, we would then have to convert the many stockbrokers who currently tend to regard anybody seeking to short the market as some form of deluded lunatic, whose aim is to undermine the very foundations of capitalism. Sadly, it is these brokers' inherently reactionary attitude that actually threatens the equilibrium of the stock market a great deal more than the prospect of some folk selling short.

Without wishing to get into laborious arguments concerning cost of carry and the like—which often dog the cash equity versus stock futures debate—I think the criticisms of the equity establishment that cash-trading would be harmed as a result of futures are largely false. Widows, orphans, and pension funds still buy Treasury Bonds for the coupon payments, even in this age of liquid futures contracts. Similarly, long-term private investors seeking a mixture of income and capital growth from their stocks would derive no benefit from buying futures alone (although their stock-switching would be assisted by narrower spreads). Pension funds would still naturally adhere to a buy-and-hold ethos, but they could derive a great deal of assistance from the trading of specific strategies against parcels of their stock and so forth.

After all, how much harm have stock index futures done to the equity market? I would wager that the detrimental effect has been somewhere significantly in the region of absolutely nothing at all. Furthermore, the benefits to cash equities have been significant—for instance, basket trades for arbitrage purposes have helped to boost the volume of cash equities.

True, when it comes to commissions then the major stockbrokers may have some cause for concern—some clients may well prefer equity futures to cash shares, thanks to the much lower charges. However, if the bid—ask spreads narrow and the stocks become more liquid, this would surely lead to sufficient extra cash business as to overwhelm any potential revenue lost.

I could go on and on. Tragically, it looks as if the arguments concerning stock futures will go on and on until some of the world's major exchanges finally decide to mobilize their organizational and marketing muscle on this front. EMU may be looming large on the horizon and cause many exchange officials to be almost myopic in their outlook until next year (and if it happens, beyond). However, in this period of an historic bull market, it seems ridiculous that perhaps the largest upswing in American and European equities we may ever witness has been entirely without even a modicum of innovation in exchange-traded derivative products. The time for individual stock futures is long overdue.

1
A Simple Q&A

This section introduces many of the key concepts concerning Single Stock Futures (SSFs) in a simple question-and-answer (Q&A) format. We list references where you can get more details on the concepts within this book. Readers determined to read our words of wisdom from cover to cover may wish to skip this section and go straight to the nitty-gritty of the editorial, but we feel this method helps as a reference to the book itself.

Q. What are SSFs?

A. Very simply they are an agreement to buy or sell a contract based on an underlying equity for settlement or delivery at a pre-specified date in the future.

Q. Why haven't we had SSFs before when there have been futures on just about everything else?

A. Well, SSFs were originally born in Amsterdam several hundred years ago, but in recent times they have not been overly popular. Some relatively peripheral exchanges listed them in the late 1980s and 1990s, but it was really only when the London-based LIFFE exchange listed their Universal Stock Futures on January 29th, 2001 that the world suddenly began to take notice of the product.

Q. But why weren't they already listed in the USA?

A. Alas, the major stumbling block in the development of SSFs was the Shad Johnson Accord, which had permitted single stock options to be traded from the early 1970s, but did not permit SSFs. The agreement was between the two US regulators (Securities Exchange Commission [SEC] and Commodities Futures Trading Commission [CFTC] for cash equities and

futures, respectively). It was only with the Commodity Futures Monderniza-
tion Act of 2000 that the way was cleared for the listing of SSFs.

Q. So, who dominates the SSF business?

A. Well, at the time of writing the most successful exchanges in the world are
in Spain (MEFF), London (well more than London as it is connected to more
than 20 countries, the London-based Euronext LIFFE), and India where the
National Stock Exchange also has a successful market.

Q. What about America?

A. The USA is coming up fast on the rails having launched SSFs in November
2002 on two exchanges: NASDAQ LIFFE (NQLX) and OneChicago. They are
expanding rapidly as we close for press, although starting from modest levels.

**Q. Yes, but isn't the very notion of stocks on individual equities just derivative
overkill?**

A. The concept that adding derivatives products is in any way harmful seems
to be at the core of this notion. True, to add derivatives to small illiquid stocks
would be counterproductive simply because price discovery in the underlying is
poor to start with (this is already established practice with options anyway).
However, the vast expansion in equities-trading during the past decade means
we have a huge pool of potential single stock futures candidates in the US and
throughout the world. Euronext LIFFE, for instance, which is the only truly
international stock futures market at the moment, has already been successfully harvesting leading global candidates from Microsoft to Telecom Italia for
its Universal Stock Futures product. In fact there are probably 1,000 or more
stocks with potential to have single stock futures listed on them in the USA
alone and probably at least 500 more in Europe at the time of writing. Add in a
further few hundred (on a conservative basis) in the rest of the world and it is
plain to see that the potential product-offerings for SSFs is quite enormous.
Essentially any stock with options listed on it already is a key candidate for an
SSF listing—which gives a significant four-figure pool of candidates throughout the world without allowing for further expansion of the options markets.

Q. But SSFs are just a big new market for speculators, right?

A. Wrong. Certainly speculative capital is involved in SSFs in the world
already. However, the flexibility for spreading (e.g., pairs-trading of two
similar stocks against each other) and the simple shorting process for futures
means that individuals or institutions, large and small, can utilize a vast
diversity of strategies to hedge their existing portfolios or future cash flows.
SSFs provide a whole new diversity and flexibility to the entire equity-trading

arena, which will arguably be more advantageous to non-speculators, even though they are very beneficial to speculators too.

Q. Well then, won't cash market volume collapse if futures are hugely successful?

A. Apart from the holistic macro-answer we gave a moment ago, one needs to consider that any market is made up of vastly more parts than just big speculators and big hedgers. Arbitrageurs and market-makers are often looking for tiny incremental profits. SSFs will, like futures, have a fair value premium calculation, which may not always be strictly represented in the price of the futures and cash markets. Such opportunities allow arbitrageurs to move in and balance the two prices; this will result in volume being reflected in both cash and derivatives markets naturally.

Q. But can't SSFs be overtraded and abused so that they detrimentally affect the cash market?

A. Another fallacy. After all, once one market gets out of whack (whether cash or futures) the arbitrageurs ought to be in on the act immediately to garner their risk-free profit and set things back in line. Given that America has long been home to many of the world's most sophisticated exchange equity derivatives operations, we would suggest that the pricing of SSFs on both OneChicago and NASDAQ LIFFE, even in their earliest days, have already tended toward the impeccably fair in this respect.

Q. Isn't the very high level of margin imposed by the SEC going to be detrimental to volumes in the US?

A. Yes, this is a key issue. In Europe, most markets have margin levels at around 10% or less. In the USA, the regulators have applied margins of 20% by regulatory fiat rather than on account of any specific risk management measure. Essentially, they are trying to appease the 50% government limit on cash stock margin, and, fair enough, 20% does look attractive by comparison with that! However, there is a key issue that competition for institutional business in the Over The Counter (OTC) market may yet provide a problem for the US SSFs business as the institutions may simply opt to transact their business OTC. Indeed, they might even opt ultimately to transact their business overseas if they find the notion of SSFs attractive and therefore look at trading in perhaps London or elsewhere in Europe where SSF margins are so much lower.

Q. Is there an opportunity for arbitrage between say a LIFFE Microsoft Universal Stock Futures (USFs) and a OneChicago Microsoft SSFs?

A. Absolutely, although there is no offset for margins. Nevertheless, similar SSFs do trade on different exchanges and arbitrage between them is possible.

However, traders need to recall that of course there may be some differences between contracts. For example, on the US market, SSFs are deliverable into the cash equity. On Euronext LIFFE, for instance, their SSFs are predominantly cash-settled. Also, each closes at a different time (Euronext LIFFE's market closes at the end of the London business day when there are several hours of trading still to go on Wall Street, for instance), which means that arbitrageurs need to have a way to close their positions out without leaving themselves open to potentially considerable basis risk.

Q. Will there eventually be an SSF on every stock?

A. No, because the key to a successful futures market involves good liquidity, and there are only a finite number of stocks with sufficient liquidity and depth that they could have a sound working relationship with a liquid future. However, as we mentioned above, the size of SSFs will likely grow considerably, even from the depressed cash equity environment prevalent in late 2002 when the US markets launched to encompass easily 1,000 or more issues in the course of the next few years from barely more than a couple of hundred at the time of writing.

Q. Why weren't SSFs invented before?

A. Well, actually they were. In Amsterdam in the 17th century, but then they fell into disuse. It has only been in recent years, as the equity markets have grown in strength and the benefits of stock index futures and options products have become plain for all to see, that the notion of SSFs once again returned to the fore.

Q. In your experience of other new markets will it take a long time for the markets to become liquid?

A. Interestingly, 20 years ago futures markets took about 18 months to become liquid and this figure has barely changed. Then, it was mostly about finding the right participants and encouraging them to trade. Nowadays, it is mostly a case that many participants have to wait until liquidity is sufficiently strong and they have received permission to deal that they can enter the market. By the time liquidity reaches initial levels, the period of time still tends to be about 18 months to two years.

Q. Is it such a good idea to have market-makers?

A. Market-makers are a good addition to any market as they are encouraged to keep bid–offer spreads tight and ensure business can be transacted in an orderly way. Certainly at Euronext LIFFE and MEFF a series of keen market-makers have been very advantageous to the product.

Q. Aren't SSFs just another tool that give the big hedge funds a way of manip- ulating the market?

A. Ah, the classic paranoia question. Alas, there isn't that much evidence of too many hedge funds actually manipulating markets in the first place. They do however have a great killer ability to make markets go their direction when they find an open wound that they can make fester some more. Truly, SSFs are just like any derivatives: they can be bought or sold and sooner or later they will settle at what the market perceives as value. In the case of the huge global corporations upon which SSFs are being based, it takes a lot more than one man or even a cabal of hedge funds to be able to move their stock permanently. Global equity market liquidity is quite considerable, and with SSFs inherently interrelated to cash equities, wondrous arbitrage opportunities will abound if the two markets get significantly out of whack.

Q. But won't SSFs just drain liquidity from the cash market?

A. Actually, the evidence remains that SSFs actually enhance liquidity in the underlying market. This has been true in commodities and perhaps most acutely in many money market instruments. In Treasury Bonds, bid–offer spreads could be as high as a big figure before Treasury Bond futures were launched, now a spread of a 32nd is taken as the absolute norm. When LIFFE launched their three-month Sterling deposit futures, there was some scepticism in the market that the cash was liquid enough to cope with the futures. In fact, the cash market found itself becoming much more deep and liquid than had ever been imagined before the LIFFE futures exchange was born. With SSFs precisely the same virtuous circle can become true.

Q. How can it benefit widows and orphans or other conservative investors who eschew derivatives?

A. Well, for a start in the cash market, the addition of SSFs tends to enhance liquidity, and, as the frictional costs (e.g., bid–offer spreads, etc.) are essentially the highest costs to be suffered by investors, it is fair to say that even without ever touching an SSF, the most conservative investors will enjoy a benefit through the cash market.

Q. What is better: cash or physical settlement?

A. A truly million dollar question. When LIFFE first moved to launch their groundbreaking international Universal Stock Futures product, they undertook a great deal of discussion with potential users in 2000. At that time, there was absolutely no clear preference for physical delivery or cash settlement among potential end-users. Nowadays, after the launch of physical delivery contracts in the USA, the barometer seems to be swinging behind increasing physical delivery. LIFFE launched their first physical delivery contracts on November 21st, 2002 to account for the fact that some settlement procedures seem to work better with physical delivery arrangements. Overall, the jury is still out, and it may be that the original LIFFE concept of cash settlement for smaller retail-oriented contracts and physical delivery for larger institutionally oriented contracts will yet gain in popularity. Right now, the entire SSFs industry needs to get sufficient liquidity into its contracts to permit rapid expansion of the product-offering—by early 2004 we expect that the physical versus cash settlement issue will be finally settled, and more than likely with physical delivery winning the day (apart from with those possible mini-contracts aimed at retail investors).

Q. Will there be options on SSFs?

A. It's a possibility, although we doubt it. Politically, the OneChicago exchange may find them difficult to list due to the shareholder structure of OneChicago where the CBOE would likely feel its core territory being invaded by OneChicago listing any such options. In the European markets, EUREX and Euronext LIFFE are the dominant options markets and the latter will probably try to concentrate on maintaining liquidity in its existing cash-settled products rather than issuing what would be an essentially identical product except for the settlement. Unlike stock futures, which provide a welcome addition to the trading of cash equities which can be difficult to sell-short for instance, options on SSFs are essentially identical to options on single stocks themselves.

Q. Will the US margin level eventually come down?

A. An interesting question. Arguably, it may go up if there is a backlash in the US marketplace in the event of a stock market sell-off for which SSFs are (unjustly) scapegoated. On the other hand, if the SSFs revolution can be seen to be a smooth process, aiding equity markets overall, then it is feasible the US regulatory desire to impose artificially high margins may yet wilt, although a lot perhaps depends on how the stockbrokers relate to the SEC. Then again, in the event that US single stock liquidity starts to seep toward foreign markets where the terms are more competitive, then one might see a very rapid pragmatic reduction in US margins at the risk of creating another Eurobond market, where London was effectively gifted a massive trading opportunity due to the US government (in this case the imposition of US withholding taxes).

Q. The contract size of 100 shares initially on the US exchanges is quite small, will the institutions muscle in and get the exchanges to raise the contract size?

A. Quite possibly. Indeed, there has long been discussion that there may be two strands of SSFs, large contracts for institutions and mini-contracts aimed predominantly at retail. These would be similar to the mini S&P contracts and full-sized S&P contracts championed by the CME in Chicago and subsequently applied to other equity index products such as the Dow Jones at the CBOT.

Q. If I go long of one SSF and go short of another in a similar sector will I get a reduced margin?

A. Yes. In fact, some of the best opportunities of all in the realm of SSFs are to be found in trading spreads between different SSFs and even other instruments such as options, index products, and even Exchange Traded Funds (ETFs). The prospect for trading "pairs" (long one, short another) SSFs alone are enormous. Whereas it can be difficult to borrow some stock you wish to sell short, this process of a futures pair can be transacted instantaneously on the same electronic platform and results in reduced margins at least in Europe—a win–win situation for all traders!

Q. Are there position limits?

A. Overall, no, although to try and reduce the possibility of squeezes in the final days before and indeed during delivery, the US exchanges do impose (quite generous) limits.

Q. Is it possible for someone to corner the market in a particular stock? What controls are there?

A. Theoroetically, the market could be cornered, but it would take an enormous amount of capital just to corner one stock. Then the possibilities of arbitrage against that stock (which would presumably now be out of balance with the rest of the market) would bring in a fresh wave of capital. Frankly, we just can't see there being anybody with sufficient resources to even conceive of such an approach. Moreover, in the digital dealing environment, the ability to measure an operation as colossal as trying to corner a major international corporation's stock would become readily apparent.

Q. Would it be possible to buy or sell more shares than are actually outstanding in a company?

A. It's quite possible, although relatively unlikely at least this early in the adoption of SSFs as a product, given the sheer size of the SSFs corporations. Nevertheless, it is not unknown in some bond markets and major options markets to habitually trade more daily volume than the underlying equity markets in the same. However, for every buyer there must be a seller, and vice versa. There is no imbalance in the actual underlying market, and position limits are there to ensure that there cannot be a huge imbalance in the number of shares to be delivered.

Q. What will happen now at "triple-witching"?

A. A good question. The simple answer is that we will have to wait and see, as the addition of deliverable SSFs in the USA at the same time as the options and index products settle means that there is another variable that may yet cause the marketplace to be squeezed. Nevertheless, the overall number of futures usually taken to delivery tends to be very modest compared with the overall volume of transactions in most physically delivered futures contracts in bond and commodity markets.

2
Basics of Single Stock Futures

On November 8th, 2002 at 10 a.m. New York time, the US Single Stock Futures market finally came alive. After years of political wrangling, having finally managed to bring an historic consensus agreement between the US futures and security regulators, the Single Stock Futures (SSFs) market arrived in the USA. A market with remarkable potential, the first day's volume was somewhat muted, but then again it was a remarkable day as both US exchanges, NASDAQ LIFFE (NQLX) and OneChicago, were electronic markets, helping to break the mould in the open outcry strongholds that dominate the US exchange landscape. Both exchanges opened simultaneously. Their first-day volumes combined to less than 10,000 lots of futures (under a million shares). Paltry volume overall, but it was the latest sign of the ongoing revolution in global equity markets, and perhaps the most important issue was that the electronic systems worked well throughout the session. Volume would grow gradually in the early days, but it was in many ways historic that SSFs had even made it to fruition ...

The SSFs revolution has had many twists in what was a fairly tortured development period, thanks mainly to US regulatory issues that precluded their listing until the passing of the US Commodity Futures Modernization Act (CFMA) (see p. 12) in 2000 during the last days of the Clinton Administration. Due to various issues, including the 09/11 tragedy, the actual introduction of SSFs in the USA was delayed, and the products only traded for the first time on November 8th, 2002, some 21 months after the CFMA was passed.

As we will see presently, SSFs have many unique facets, but they are a simple futures contract just like their cousins in commodities and financial markets et al.

In the first year of trading, volumes have been somewhat muted but, against a background of a bear market in the underlying market, derivatives innovation has always been difficult. The fact remains that SSFs are poised to become a powerhouse product in forthcoming years.

FUTURES

The origins of modern futures markets can be traced back several hundred years, although the most commonly noted starting point is the launch of forward corn-trading on March 13th, 1851 at the Chicago Board Of Trade (CBOT) (which had originally been founded in 1848). The modern financial futures market first rose to prominence in the 1970s in the wake of the collapse of the Bretton Woods agreement with the US abandoning the Gold Standard leading to the free floating of foreign exchange markets.

Nevertheless, it is a tricky issue to precisely define where modern "futures" truly began, as, for example, forward rice contracts were traded in Osaka in 1730. Equity derivatives markets bear their modern origins in the establishment of the Chicago Board Options Exchange in 1973. CBOE has remained the largest single stock options exchange in the USA ever since, although it is nowadays under considerable competitive pressure from the all-electronic International Securities Exchange (ISE), a relative newcomer to the options market, established in just 1997, that started trading in late May 2000. The other leading US options markets are the Philadelphia Stock Exchange, The Pacific Coast Exchange (in San Francisco) and the New York-based American Stock Exchange (AMEX).

The first equity futures were index products launched initially at the Kansas City Board of Trade in February 1982. The KCBOT launched a stock index future on the Value Line index, now based upon some 1,650 US shares, over 70% traded on the New York Stock Exchange, some 20% on the NASDAQ, and the remainder on the AMEX and Canadian markets. The Chicago Mercantile soon managed to gain a leading market share in stock index futures after launching futures based upon the S&P 500 index in April 1982. The S&P 500, a leading benchmark for US equity prices, popular with US fund-managers, quickly established itself as the benchmark US index for futures markets. Other stock indices have been listed on exchanges throughout the rest of the world during the past 20 years. Most successful stock index futures/options have tended to be based on local markets, although following the introduction of the euro in 12 nations of the European Union (EU), pan-European indices, most notably the Dow Jones EUROSTOXX 50, have become popular combining equities from throughout the EU. Elsewhere regional stock indices have so far failed to make a big impact on futures markets.[1]

The period leading up to the launch of equity index futures in 1982 was notable as there was a fundamental regulatory conflict in the USA. The Secur-

---

[1] Indeed, even pan-European indices have had a very chequered life until recently. The LIFFE FTSE Eurotrack contracts from the late 1980s were unable to attract much interest, and it has only been with the birth of the euro that there is even a remote European consciousness—albeit still embryonic—developing for cross-border investing.

ities and Exchange Commission (SEC) had been created from the Securities Exchange Act in 1934 in the wake of the Wall Street Crash of 1929. It reports to the US House of Representatives Finance Committee. Meanwhile, the Commodity Futures Trading Commission (CFTC) had been established more recently in 1974 and reports to the Agriculture Committee, as it had its origins in the commodity business. However, as financial deregulation helped the futures markets to grow explosively, the balance of power in volume terms switched to financial products. By 1982, the futures exchanges wanted to list index futures, and a meeting of the two chairmen of the regulatory bodies was convened to reach an agreement on the regulation of those instruments that both regulatory bodies could reasonably claim they had a right to oversee. The end result was the Shad–Johnson Accord named after SEC Chairman John Shad and Philip McBride Johnson, the Chairman of the CFTC. This agreement allowed the launch of equity index products. Single stock futures, however, remained illegal in the USA until the CFMA was enabled in 2000.

SSFs, had already been listed on various world exchanges during the 1990s. The Sydney Futures Exchange paved the way in 1994 soon followed by the Hong Kong Futures Exchange (now merged into what has become Hong Kong Exchange) in 1995. Various other exchanges followed suit in the mid- to late 1990s, including OM in Sweden and markets as far afield as South Africa, South America, and Russia.

It was only when LIFFE introduced their Universal Stock Futures (USFs) project at a press conference on September 20th, 2000 (although there had been a press release five days earlier) that SSFs moved to centre stage in the priorities of the world's exchanges. The US movement to have SSFs made legal became vitally important for the futures markets, particularly in Chicago, although initially the US options industry, notably the CBOE were against the proposal to introduce SSFs citing the fact that the products could already be constructed synthetically on their marketplaces.[2]

On September 20th, the CME and CBOT jointly responded to LIFFE's historic declaration of their intention to launch international SSFs by noting:

> LIFFE's announcement that it will trade single stock futures on five U.S. securities is the best possible evidence of the unfair competition the U.S. futures exchanges face today. LIFFE will trade … a product we are banned by Federal statute from trading … We fully understand the need to protect one's competitive position and the tendency to protect one's turf but when that behaviour affects the best interests of the United States, it is indefensible.

---

[2] However, as we will see, Bill Brodsky, the CBOE chief executive officer (CEO), ultimately threw his weight and influence behind the product and would be pivotal in the moves to create OneChicago.

Box 2.1   The Shad–Johnson Accord and the CFMA

In 1982 with the introduction of index futures and the possibility that there could be single stock futures and individual equity options, there loomed the problem over whether these instruments would be futures or security instruments. This was a classic power struggle not just for influence but for funds. At the time the responsibilities and hence the budgets being doled out were increasing. This was the time when futures contract volumes had increased significantly, and financial futures especially. It was seen by both the SEC (who regulated the securities markets) and the CFTC (who regulated the futures markets) that whoever won this battle would be kingpin, get a huge increase in funds, and could eventually be in a position to take the other organization over; a classic, government interdepartmental turf war in other words . . .

There were various unsuccessful attempts to patch things up in the intervening years, but these failed because one regulator would be likely to end up a loser. Similarly, politicians on the Agriculture Committee were unwilling to suddenly give away one of their prize possessions—the CFTC—(despite agricultural products being a minuscule proportion of total futures volume), and naturally the Banking Committee simply could not see why it didn't hold sway over the entire realm of financial products. Interestingly, the CFTC itself had been born in 1974 with some opposition from the Treasury, who believed they had the sole right to regulate foreign exchange and bond market products . . .

Eventually, after surviving some 18 years, the Shad–Johnson Accord was finally dismantled through the Clinton Administration's CFMA of 2000, after extensive lobbying from US futures exchanges when suddenly the threat to their turf was increasingly coming from overseas (and predominantly European exchanges). Chairmen Arthur Levitt of the SEC and Bill Rainer of CFTC presided over the historic agreement to break down the Shad–Johnson Accord. Although, interestingly, it remained a moot point whether Shad–Johnson had ever been the permanent ban on SSFs it was later interpreted to be or rather initially was a waypost (signpost) to agreeing stock index futures with a view to agreeing SSFs at some subsequent juncture . . . but once again that old regulatory turf war seemed to preclude any progress for 18 years.

The CFMA essentially provides for joint jurisdiction between the CFTC and SEC over SSFs and narrow-based indices (collectively defined as Security Futures). The CFTC retains exclusive US jurisdiction over broad-based stock index futures. Under the agreement, the CFTC is primary regulator of futures markets and futures commission merchants, while the SEC is primary regulator of securities markets and broker–dealers. To trade security futures, all markets and their brokers must file registration with the opposite regulator (i.e., futures brokers and futures exchanges with the SEC, stockbrokers and stock exchanges with the CFTC).

Former CFTC Chairman Philip McBride Johnson admitted in 2000 that Shad–Johnson was an attempt to maintain jurisdiction over the futures market as a whole, arguing that "if futures contracts are regulated based on the underlying asset they track, then the industry would be faced with scores of different regulators." Naturally, the SEC would have liked to have jurisdiction because of the impact it could have on the securities and options markets. In this respect, it will be interesting to see how the joint sovereignty agreement for SSFs between the CFTC and SEC will ultimately work out.

No sooner had LIFFE launched their USF product than suddenly there was a groundswell of opinion in the US exchanges that the Shad–Johnson Accord was restricting capitalist expression and that the US markets had to be permitted to offer the product as soon as possible. Under the reformist futures regulatory regime of Chairman William Rainer at the CFTC, the SEC soon became convinced of the merits of SSFs after much wrangling in Congress.

Nevertheless, it took a lot of extensive lobbying before the US politicians finally gave their approval. The end result was a system whereby both the CFTC and SEC had a degree of joint sovereignty over the product, and indeed some regulations are applied differently to market participants dependent on whether they have a securities or futures background:

> The proposed framework is intended to promote innovation, maintain US competitiveness, reduce systemic risk, and protect derivatives customers. Any proposal ultimately adopted will not be tailored to the desires of any special interest or driven by any jurisdictional concerns. We want to find solutions that serve the public interest.
>
> C. Robert Paul, then General Counsel CFTC
> (and now General Counsel to OneChicago)
> testifying before the US Senate Committee on Agriculture,
> Nutrition, and Forestry, March 20th, 2000

Meanwhile, back in Europe, the Spanish MEFF exchange actually launched their SSFs slightly ahead of LIFFE on January 11th, 2001 and quickly established very strong volumes. The exchange remained the largest SSFs market in the world before the US markets launched in late 2002.

Subsequently, the first North American SSFs were launched on Canadian Telecom company, Nortel, by the Bourse de Montreal on January 31st, 2001, with a roadshow in Montreal and Toronto where the co-author of this book, Patrick L. Young, was a keynote speaker promoting the product.[3]

---

[3] Alas, the major Canadian stock of the hour was Nortel and it subsequently suffered the fate of so many telecom companies by losing a vast amount of value and becoming much less of a glamour stock. Unfortunate timing for the Bourse de Montreal, who subsequently placed more emphasis on their interesting BOX joint venture with market-maker Timberhill and the Boston Stock Exchange to trade options and perhaps other equity derivatives. On the other hand, cynics might argue that having Patrick Young promote your product is a death sentence, although the author would claim LIFFE's USFs in his defence, which he vigourously championed on the various LIFFE roadshows ...

However, with the CFMA being signed by President Clinton on December 21st, 2000, the battle for US exchange supremacy began with a great deal of jostling for position. Essentially every exchange, from the predators through the prey to the roadkill of US bourses, suddenly expressed an interest in joining the single stock futures bandwagon. CBOE CEO Bill Brodsky commented to the Investment Analysts Society of Chicago on March 1st: "We not only plan to trade the product, we intend to dominate the field" (Greenberg, 2002).

Then on 26th March, 2001, Sir Brian Williamson, LIFFE's Chairman stole another march on his rivals with an historic deal to create a joint venture for profit exchange (now permissible under the CFMA where they had previously been restricted). Williamson, a former Governor of the National Association of Securities Dealers (NASD), announced a new joint venture with Frank Zarb, Chairman of NASDAQ, to create NASDAQ LIFFE markets, an exchange aiming to provide SSFs in the US marketplace. The already success-ful LIFFE Connect system would be the chosen platform and NASDAQ's leverage in the US equity market would complement the technological abilities of the LIFFE team, as well as their experience in developing their international USF products.

The reaction in Chicago was one of initial surprise, which gave way to perhaps the best example of exchange co-operation ever seen in the windy city. Within weeks, on 14th May, 2001, a press conference announced the establishment of what would ultimately be christened OneChicago, a joint venture with 40% shareholdings for the CME and CBOE, while the CBOT would hold 10% and staff the remaining 10%. Subsequently, the OneChicago board would also announce the appointment of former CFTC Chairman Bill Rainer as Chairman and CEO of the exchange. The addition of former CFTC General Counsel Bob Paul as General Counsel for OneChicago meant the architects of the CFTC's regulatory reforms would now become primary movers in making SSFs a reality. OneChicago implemented a system based upon the CBOE direct match engine coupled to some technology applications developed by CME.

Several other US exchanges have suggested intentions to enter the SSFs arena, including the New York based AMEX and NYMEX, as well as the proposed Island Futures Exchange. The latter appeared to be a mothballed project by late 2002, while NYMEX also appeared to have abandoned short-term plans to enter SSFs. AMEX was still suggesting it may launch SSFs, although it would be a rather unique figure in the marketplace, as it has suggested it would use open outcry trading on the exchange floor as opposed to the electronic trading approach preferred by all the other leading SSFs exchanges worldwide. Given the cost of establishing floor-trading operations and the fact that it is unlikely open outcry is going to survive much longer as a primary method of futures/options dealing (it is already to all intents and purposes extinct in Europe and Asia, for instance), the AMEX concept of floor-trading seemed a little eccentric. Given that the launched US exchanges were listing anything from 15 to 20 or more new contracts a week in their early weeks during late 2002, it seems impossible to believe that a floor-based operation could manage to cope with the sheer speed with which the electronic markets could operate.

HISTORICAL ORIGINS

However, SSFs have in fact got some significant historical precedents and their genuine origins lie as far back to the first half of the 17th century, when effectively they were traded in Amsterdam. The story of how the stock of the East India Company (first issued in 1602), was traded in 17th century Amsterdam is contained in *Confusión de Confusiones* by Joseph de la Vega, originally published in 1688 (Fridson et al., 1996). Joseph de la Vega was a Sephardic Jew born in Portugal whose family had moved to Amsterdam where a significant coterie of Jewish traders, among many, played the stock market. In his book, de la Vega delightfully paints a picture of the stock market in a fashion which is perhaps alarmingly similar to the marketplace of today. He describes in some detail how the market had developed from the simple trading in stock to all the means by which traders, speculators, brokers, and even the money-lenders developed means of trading to cope with debilitating volatility and the impediment of ineffective regulation. The emergence of 'short-selling', its prohibition, and the development of forward contracts in an effort to hedge positions. The introduction of options, not just simple put and call options but even 'straddles'. Every which way was employed by the innovative Amsterda-mers to trade in the stock of not only the East India Company but also the later West India Company. Such was the volatility and high value of an individual share that they even traded a mini-contract, named "ducaton", trades which effectively traded a tenth of the value of a full share. The book is a delight and a great lesson in how, while everything has changed, nothing is different. The book takes the form of four dialogues representing different characters involved with the market. The Shareholder is the first character and, when asked to describe "the market", he offers the following:

> ... this enigmatic business which is at once the fairest and most deceitful in Europe, the noblest and the most infamous in the world, the finest and the most vulgar on earth. It is a quintessence of academic learning and a paragon of fraudulence; it is a touchstone for the intelligent and a tombstone for the audacious, a treasury of usefulness and a source of disaster ...

If only he could see it now.

WHAT IS A SINGLE STOCK FUTURE?

It would be impossible to have a guide to SSFs without introducing the basics of futures contracts. Readers who may find themselves rendered utterly incandescent by yet another definition of the basics of futures contracts are requested to indulge the authors their moment of explanation for novices, and skip to p. 19.

BASIC PRINCIPLES OF FUTURES CONTRACTS

Futures, as the name suggests, are instruments for pricing forward a market. In other words, a contract is agreed to either take delivery of, or to supply, a contract based upon a future settlement date. Such a contract can be based on almost any underlying instrument. At the time of writing, products based upon all manner of commodities, foreign exchange, money market, and bonds already exist along with various equity products. Everything from the result of the next American football game (on Tradesports.com) to the weather (at various exchanges including Euronext LIFFE and the CME) are available as tradable futures contracts. The concept of commoditizing a market to create a forward-priced instrument for future settlement can essentially be applied to any tangible or intangible good.

A forward price is one based upon some future delivery or settlement of a product. In other words, if we want to buy something now we would expect to pay less than we would for delivery at some predetermined date in the future because, of course, there are various issues to consider that affect the price such as (but not limited to) inflation and the cost to the seller of holding the product, not forgetting the forgone utility of what could be gained from the cash in the meantime, etc. In futures markets, there is usually a predetermined "fair value" calculation that is employed to arrive at the price likely to be demanded for a futures contract. We will look at fair value later with specific regard to SSFs.

A futures contract essentially prices a commodity for future settlement. Contracts are generally of a standard size, allowing traders to enter and exit trades with ease. Traders can just as easily enter (or exit) a position through buying or selling a futures contract. Traditional equity investors may find it difficult to conceive of just why anybody would seek to sell something they may not already own; but, in fact, it can have significant benefits as we will see in the trading sections of this book by permitting spread trades, as well as allowing investors to benefit from an overbought position in an equity, which when it readjusts to a more reasonable value can garner a profit for the trader. The major difference between conventional buy and hold investors and futures-traders is that the latter group tend to be more flexible in terms of their positions. Not only do futures-traders tend to have a shorter time horizon, they are also much more open to buying or selling markets.

Trading on futures exchanges uses a central clearing process provided by a clearing house. This is very beneficial for all market participants as trades are matched by the clearing house, which effectively becomes the counterparty to each and every trade. In other words, the clearing house takes on the risk that if you buy an SSF and your buyer defaults on their position, then you are not penalized. This is perhaps the greatest reason why trading futures can actually help you to sleep at night, as opposed to keeping you awake! Any futures trade that keeps you awake at night is likely because you have a wrong position or too much risk in your own account, not as a result of systemic risks in the marketplace!

All futures positions use margin. There are several components to margin. When you open a position (either by buying or selling, remember), then the clearing house will request that you post initial margin through your broker. This represents a form of deposit on your purchase, and in the US marketplace for example is 20% of the underlying value of the stock. The clearing house of course levies this on both parties to any transaction, so it immediately garners a deposit of 40% on the position. Thereafter, every time the price moves, a variation margin is posted on the traders account, meaning he must be able to cover his losses in advance of actually closing the position. This can also be referred to as "marking to market". To be precise, a "variation margin" can even be imposed above and beyond the level of the marking to market in order to ensure the clearing house is confident that all participants have adequate coverage in their accounts for a market that may be highly volatile. In exceptional circumstances (e.g., during the equity market crash of October 1987), it is commonplace for the clearing house to levy additional margin to ensure that the market has adequate capitalization.

All futures contracts have a finite end date. Traditionally, futures are listed on a quarterly expiration cycle: March, June, September, and December. Sometimes serial months are also used—in the case of many SSFs serial months are listed.

In the case of SSFs, almost all markets are traded electronically, meaning that traders' orders can be routed electronically directly to the exchange (via the broker's exchange connection) without having to be entered by a broker, presuming you have a suitable direct dealing connection.

BASIC PRINCIPALS OF SINGLE STOCK FUTURES

SSFs are, as their name suggests, based upon an individual security issue (hence the popular American identifier of Security Futures). Therefore, each SSF has an underlying issue (e.g., Microsoft) that essentially dictates the price of the future. There are various other determinants of the price. A core issue is the concept of fair value. Put simply, a stock future is a contract to buy or sell shares of a particular company at a predetermined date in the future. Fair value is a measure of the opportunity cost of holding a futures position compared with the return one could garner from an essentially riskless instrument (namely, a short-term, typically three-month, Government Treasury Bill [T-Bill]) and the impact of dividends on the share. Therefore fair value is calculated first by adding the value of the expected T-Bill return to the price of the cash stock for the appropriate time period. Then, if a dividend is payable during the life of the contract one subtracts the expected value of the dividend from the cash share price plus T-Bill return figure. Put simply, fair value on a stock is its current cash price plus the opportunity cost of not investing cash in Treasuries minus the dividend the stock pays; that is:

$$\text{Futures value} = \text{Stock price} + \text{Interest} - \text{Dividend}$$

In calculating this equation, the current T-Bill rate is always used for interest, and it ought to be noted that therefore applicable broker margin rates may differ significantly from this Bill yield.

So, to hold a stock for six months, we could trade a forward futures contract and buy T-bills in our account using 95% of the face value as margin. This effectively would offset some of the forward premium. Dividends would not matter because they are subtracted, so we would be able to buy a stock with two-to-one leverage and hold the position for six months with a final net cost of about 2.5% per year in premium. This is compared with a broker rate that may be as high as say 8% during the same underlying economic conditions, which at two-to-one leverage means that borrowing half the money would cost you 4% per year.

An SSF, thanks to the expected added return from the Bill return, will therefore tend to have a premium above the cash value of the underlying equity. Naturally, as the share comes closer to expiry this price will tend to converge. If it didn't, then there would be an arbitrage profit on expiry for the trader who sold SSFs and bought underlying shares. Of course, in the marketplace, fair value is an important issue, and, when an SSF drops significantly below fair value or rises significantly above this level, arbitrageurs will enter the market to offset this price disparity with a view to undoing the position when the market gets back toward fair value. Of course, the issue with fair value isn't quite so simply cut and dried as basically selling when the market rises just above fair value or falls below it. In practice, the share in question has to move a reasonable distance away from fair value for it to be profitably arbitraged. Why? Well, for a start, there is the issue of the bid–offer spread, which applies to both the cash equity and the SSFs. That's going to mean the fair value level has to be exceeded by at least several cents to allow for a profitable entry and indeed to permit a profitable exit too, if the trader doesn't want to hold the position until expiry.

Of course, sometimes, when a market is moving very rapidly due to recent news or overall market activity, such volatility may also lead the fair value to range quite substantially, but market practitioners may be simply too busy (or too concerned about the execution risk of being left with an unhedged position on one or other side of the trade) to actually want to arbitrage the position.

Nevertheless, SSFs traders ought to always be abreast of the fair value levels of any stocks they are tracking. If nothing else, when you want to sell a single stock future, if you can see a share which is slightly above its fair value, you might as well try to capitalize by gaining a slight edge to your position ... Also, don't forget that if a large dividend is expected then an SSF may actually be trading at a discount to the underlying cash equity. If you want to buy the market with a view toward a pure capital gain, this can provide an additional edge to your position when entering the market. Finally, never forget that the impact of a share's dividend is not felt on the payment date, but on the date it goes "ex-dividend" in the stock market (i.e., the day the shares are no longer traded with the right to the dividend). It is on this day that the dividend factored into the pricing of an SSF ought to be evened out with the underlying share, although of course the impact of the return from T-Bills will remain in the price of the future compared with the stock.

DIFFERENCES BETWEEN OWNING STOCK AND FUTURES

There are several key differences to owning an SSF and owning the actual underlying share (Table 2.1).

Table 2.1

Cash		Future
Yes	Voting rights	No
Yes	Dividend	No
Yes	Ownership period: can be infinite as long as the company stays in business	No
No	Expires with the end of contract or if the company closes or is taken over	Yes

KEY DIFFERENCES BETWEEN TRADING SINGLE STOCK FUTURES AND CASH EQUITIES

Those used to the specialist systems of the US stock markets will find the fact that their orders can be shown in the open market (similar to the price priority already exercised by many overseas equity systems, on Euronext, for instance) a novelty. Essentially, the best orders must be shown to the market, and, at present, ECNs[4] and other order internalization processes are not commonplace in the futures market transaction chain. Moreover, speed of execution through the electronic marketplaces, which predominate in SSF exchanges, means that execution speeds will be very swift compared with the open outcry equity markets of New York (presuming your order actually ever hits the floor of the NYSE—the percentage of retail business that ever actually gets transacted on the floor of Wall Street is a fairly low percentage of the overall trade there).

SSF exchanges tend to have their liquidity provided by a judicious mix of individual speculators (known as "locals"), specialist market-makers, and banks or other significant financial institutions. Nevertheless, in electronic trading, orders are usually subject to what is known as Time Price priority, also called the FIFO system. Standing for "First In First Out", FIFO means that orders placed earlier will be executed ahead of those placed at a later stage. There are some subtle idiosyncrasies in this system that permit specific order types such as block and spread trades, but overall the playing field for futures orders is remarkably flat for plain vanilla futures traders.

Block-trading remains somewhat of a bone of contention. The traditional floor-trader view in the likes of the Chicago pits (one of the few places where traditional pits remain) is that block-trading is a bad thing because it is given an unfair priority ahead of the hard working locals who try to provide liquidity in the pits. The locals have a point, but then again block trades happen all the time Over the Counter (OTC). By allowing them to take place on exchange, traders can glimpse where the really heavy volume is occurring.

STAMP DUTY

In the UK, purchasers of cash equities still pay one of the world's more regressive taxes—"stamp duty"—on every transaction. This does not apply to SSFs in any respect (even if Euronext LIFFE or a rival exchange were to introduce physically delivered futures), making them a much more cash-

---

[4] ECNs, or Electronic Communications Networks, hailed by many as a solution to issues of equity dealing, are in fact mostly a carbuncle that is a symptom of the problems rather than a solution *per se*. They provided electronic matching of trades that are then booked/settled on a conventional stock exchange.

efficient trading tool, albeit as a result of the short-sighted nature of the UK Exchequer, which continues to harm investment returns through this duty.

THE UPTICK RULE

The financial and industrial world has been afflicted with termites as insidious and destructive as the insect termites. Instead of feeding on wood they feed and thrive on other people's money ... these financial termites are those who practice the art of predatory or high finance. They destroy the legitimate function of finance and become a common enemy of investors and businesses ... one of the chief characteristics of such finance has been its inhumanity, its disregard of social and human values.

William O. Douglas, SEC Chairman in a speech circa 1938

In the wake of the Wall Street Crash of 1929, President Roosevelt set about reforming a great deal of the US financial system. The Securities Exchange Act of 1934 established the SEC. It was the third of three major securities acts following on from the Securities Act (1933), which aimed to increase market accountability and disclosure of stock issues, and "Glass Steagall", which separated investment-banking from retail banking.

A primary element of the remit of the SEC was specifically to regulate short sales of exchange-listed securities in order to prevent perceived abuses in short-selling, which many people blamed for causing the crash in the first place. The SEC studied the situation for several years and their short-selling regulations were created in 1937. There are three core elements to the short-selling regulations:

(i)   allowing relatively unrestricted short selling in an advancing market;
(ii)   preventing short selling at successively lower prices, thus eliminating short selling as a tool for driving the market down; and
(iii)   preventing short sellers from accelerating a declining market by exhausting all remaining bids at one price level, causing successively lower prices to be established by long sellers.

L. C. Gupta (2002)

A core element of the SEC rules is the so-called "uptick rule". In other words, the market cannot be sold short unless the last trade has been at least the same price as the previous trade and preferably above the previous trade. Therefore, a cash equity market cannot be sold short if the market has recently ticked down in price. This is of course a considerably restrictive issue for traders in contemporary markets. While the law exists in the USA, the UK stock market, for example, has never been burdened with any such regulation (at least not this century: the LSE got its period of short-selling regulation over and done with many years ago) and has managed to survive as a leading centre of cash equity liquidity.

SSFs are not subject to this constraint, any trader can enter a position by selling short on an up- or downtick Overall, therefore, SSFs allow a much fairer and open market in equities, as price discovery can be achieved without any artificial restraints on price. Of course, sellers of SSFs need to recall that if the contracts are physically delivered, then they may be liable to deliver stock if they hold the contracts until they expire.

SHORT-SELLING[5]

> Professional short sellers don't start out betting against the Little
> League teams, rooting for earthquakes and plane crashes, or doubting
> the tooth fairy at an early age. They don't fly the British flag on the
> Fourth of July, wear black at weddings and white at funerals, or
> douse apple pie with Tabasco sauce ... Known short sellers suffer the
> same reputation as the detested bat. They're reviled as odious pests,
> smudges on the walls of Wall Street, pecuniary vampires who suck
> profits out of healthy stocks until those stocks are too weak to stand
> up in the market.
>
> John Rothchild (1998)

Among the many mails received on SSFs-related issues, one bubbling up to the surface on a regular basis concerns that thorny old issue of short-selling. Indeed, short-selling has long been pilloried by many folk in the USA, and this is likely to remain a controversial issue for some time to come. Yet, we are happy to contend that short-selling is not merely a natural and beneficial process for markets but indeed it also helps financial markets much more than it actually harms them. A great many people view SSFs from rather polar extremes: "they're terrific because they mean we can short sell with ease and impunity" or "they're the product of Beelzebub encouraging anti-patriotic folk to destroy wealth."

The reality, like many such polarizations, actually lies somewhere in-between. Indeed, the explosion in issues of SSFs in recent years heralds a

---

[5] This section is based on articles Patrick Young originally contributed to http:// www.appliederivatives.com in his groundbreaking *Single Stock Futures Guide*, which was sponsored by LIFFE during the period 2000–2002.

great new opportunity to ensure that prices more accurately reflected valuations of a company and indeed market sentiment in those stocks.

In essence, there are a series of key arguments concerning short-selling that impact significantly upon how the world at large is going to view the ongoing growth in SSFs products in forthcoming years. It is therefore worth running through several key arguments in this chapter both as an *aide-mémoire* for SSFs proponents and as a good reference point for those cynical about the benefits of SSFs as a multidirectional trading tool:

1. The unpatriotic argument

> Now let me clear the air on another common fallacy that some people hold ... Some think being a bear and/or selling short is in some way unpatriotic or negative. They believe that to invest your money in the industry of your country and to lose it is more patriotic than to "sell those industries short" by selling their stock short ... because you feel we have entered a bear market.
>
> Harry Schultz (2002)

Put simply, nobody wishes to destroy their country, but the first concern of every citizen must be to ensure they can feed, clothe, and house themselves and their families. If the marketplace is going down, then you must be willing to sell short, and SSFs are the cheapest, simplest, and most efficient way to do that on an exchange. Few people would argue against the concept of a safety net, to safeguard those who have fallen upon hard times, being provided by the government to help keep people from falling into severe poverty. However, the notion that, by failing to protect yourself from the ravages of a bear phase or major bear market you are in some way being patriotic, is surely a highly flawed notion. All traders owe it to themselves and their families to remain solvent in financial markets.

Moreover, hanging on in a bear market—or even a bear phase or a bearish sector—not only endangers your wealth but it also leaves you with less money to invest at the bottom of the next cycle. After all, Nathan Rothschild noted long ago that the time to buy was when "blood is on the streets", and, frankly, if that's your blood seeping into the gutters you aren't really in much of a position to do anything except to perhaps try some patriotic begging on street corners or patriotically claiming welfare benefits.

The unpatriotic tag is often linked to the argument, still thought credible in some circles, that ultimately it was:

2. Short-selling is what caused the 1929 crash

True, President Hoover was convinced a bearish conspiracy had sunk the market, but his own raft of Senatorial inquisitions and a multiplicity of detailed studies proved this simply was not the case (although that didn't stop the political classes enshrining the SEC with a mandate to reduce short-selling, which duly led to the Short Selling regulations of 1937). Indeed, the amount of stock sold short during 1929 amounted to about one-eighth of 1% of all shares outstanding. Not enough surely to sink any major capitalist marketplace, least of all the Wall Street colossus of the roaring twenties. Let's move on to another fallacy:

3. Short sellers need to be restricted, and therefore SSFs are a bad thing because they allow uncontrolled sales of shares

If short selling had a warning label, it would read: SHORT SELLING IS REWARDING ON OCCASION. IT CAN BE HABIT-FORMING AND POTENTIALLY RUINOUS TO WEALTH.

John Rothchild (1998)

Short-selling is just another tool in the trader's armoury. Few folk—even the most elementary golfers—want to go around a golf course with just a putter or a wedge, and likewise we would all scorn the tennis professional who doesn't believe in playing any backhand shots. Yet, for some reason, there is a strong feeling among many folk that short-selling is somehow more dangerous a practice than simply buying stocks and hanging on for dear life until they either prosper or go bankrupt.

True, there are some things that do make short-selling cash shares more risky, such as the "uptick rule" introduced in the USA toward the nadir of the 1930s' bear market, restricting short sales to every time the market ticks up. Intriguingly, value-hunting buyers are not restricted to only buying stock every time the share price ticks down, which one could argue would help people avoid being caught up in bubbles such as the dotcom mania of recent years.

The very concept of short-sellers needing to be restricted is fallacious reasoning. In an information-transparent stock market environment, there is no reason that short-selling should be restricted. Indeed, a healthy cosmopolitan mix of buyers and sellers in derivatives markets has only improved liquidity in underlying cash markets everywhere else, and the resulting price enhancements have benefited everybody in the marketplace overall, by reducing frictional costs and making for an easier transactional environment. SSFs play a key role in helping make sure the cash stock market is better "policed", in terms of providing fair value. Similarly, by being simple to transact without the hassle of requiring borrowing of stock for delivery, etc., the SSFs market is a very neat way to sell short for hedging purposes whether as an interpolation or against an existing portfolio. Nevertheless, nothing will stop bubbles emerging, and extremes will always happen in markets, because that reflects a fundamental facet of human nature. The ability to judiciously sell short without restriction can help maintain liquidity. However, there are those who would argue:

4. Short-selling individual equities makes downward movements greater

Actually, this is quite abjectly incorrect, as short-selling (through cash or derivative markets) actually provides a degree of "buoyancy" to a falling market. Short-sellers have to buy back sooner or later, and toward major market bottoms where the stock market may be sliding often the only buyers providing support are short-sellers covering their losses. As Wall Street veteran Phil Carret has noted:

> Near the bottom of a market, when pessimism has triumphed and nobody wants to buy stocks, the only buyers are short sellers covering their positions. Without them, the people who want to unload their stocks would have nobody to sell to.

Similarly, Harry Schultz notes:

> The short seller contributes mightily to the creation of more orderly and stabilized markets through the demand for and the supply of securities he creates. In bull markets and bear, he is selling short, and he is eventually "covering" (i.e. buying) which demand puts a cushion under market declines. Without the short seller, our markets would be bottomless, - those times when panic prevails and bulls rush for the exits while the short seller is calmly buying stock to cover his shorts and taking a profit.

Certainly, there is a welter of evidence that stock index futures can help calm extreme moves, through giving traders the flexibility to buy or sell. This is replicated at the micro level of individual shares by SSFs.

5. Short-selling destroys value

By selling an SSF or shorting a cash stock, we are merely speculating on the likely price outcome of a particularly share. By selling Microsoft, for instance, nobody is actually stealing anything from Bill Gates's empire or forcing people to cut back their business expenditure. Indeed, where businesses can exhibit fine economic fundamentals, the short-seller will be driven out at a loss. However, to have only one-sided trading (i.e., buy only or buying with restricted selling) is in itself an impediment to efficient price discovery.

Indeed, it is interesting to note that where the whole process of short-selling has been banned—e.g., in the USA during 1931—(when the "uptick" rule was also created) and at one time or another in many other nations, such as Britain, France, and Japan—this has usually been close to a major market bottom ...

SHORT-SELLING CONCLUSION

> A bear market is a bull market in gestation.
>
>   Anonymous

The most significant thing one needs to consider when it comes to short-selling is that during cycles of bear and bull markets everybody needs to maintain all the tools for the job. The gardener who uses a lawnmower to deadhead his flowers will look as foolish as a trader who avoids employing judicious short positions in all markets, but especially in SSFs when they find there are pressing reasons to believe they can best preserve their profit-and-loss account by selling short.

> Bullish fund managers meet over lunch or swap stock picks on the phone and during coffee breaks at conferences, but nobody accuses them of conspiring to drive stock prices up. Get two short sellers in an elevator and it's an automatic conspiracy to drive prices down ... If short selling were more widespread and various obstacles were removed, then we might see more happy faces during bear markets.

The good news is that SSFs provide precisely that degree of flexibility to the benefit of traders throughout the world. Indeed:

> Nowhere will the advantage of SSFs be more pronounced than in the transaction facilitation and interest rate cost savings involved in the short selling of stock.
>
>   NQLX, *Single Stock Futures for the Professional Trader*
>   (http://www.nqlx.com)

Quite frequently, one of the biggest problems facing the short-seller can be the problem of actually borrowing stock to match up to their short sale obligations. Searching through stock loan departments for stocks that are difficult or indeed all but impossible to borrow is not merely frustrating for the wannabe short-seller, it also potentially impedes the smooth running of capital markets. Being unable to locate stock can provoke a short squeeze, which hardly helps promote more efficient stock markets. With SSFs, the supply of short futures can expand infinitely as they are a function of open interest rather than being reliant on the supply of cash stock, which may be tightly held. Thus price discovery can be achieved using SSFs in a way that is currently not possible with tightly held and/or difficult-to-borrow stocks.

WHICH MONTH TO TRADE?

While it may seem sensible to always try and trade the SSFs with the longest period to expiry, in reality, trading tends to be concentrated on what is known as the front month. This will usually be the month closest to expiry—although in the last month of a contract's life, the market tends to "rollover" to the next nearest month as expiry approaches. The best thing most futures traders can do is always ensure they follow liquidity, because trading in illiquid months can mean you receive worse price fills as a result of bid–offer spreads being wider (and having smaller available size). Rollovers—the process of moving from one contract month to the next—is commonplace and can usually be achieved at a very low cost if you want to maintain a position for more than a couple of months.

THE ARGUMENTS FOR AND AGAINST SINGLE STOCK FUTURES

There has been much debate on the merits and benefits of introducing SSFs. It is heartening to note that in a world with unparalleled availability of coherent information, thanks to digital highways such as the Internet, the debate on the merits of SSFs has often been dominated by detractors who seem to have only the barest concept of the product. Having said that, some very coherent criticism remains, although getting that message across seems to take longer on some continents than others:

> Sooner or later they will get round to launching single stock futures (SSFs) in the US. Judging by the repeated delays, and the response to those delays, a lot of people evidently think this is a very big deal. But is the fuss justified? God did not create SSFs; was there any need to invent them?

> Mark Beddis (2002)[6]

Obviously, the launching of SSFs in late November 2002 in the USA was the acid test for the product. It is not unreasonable to suggest that if they cannot thrive in the world's foremost capitalist country then they will not flourish anywhere. On the other hand, the history of SSFs has been remarkably chequered to date. The launch of SSFs in Hong Kong by the HKFE was

---

[6] Our thanks to Mark for his article, which remains one of the most coherent contra-SSF pieces around. We are happy to borrow from his arguments within this section of the book, even if we disagree with his standpoint!

seen as a remarkably brave attack on the Stock Exchange of Hong Kong (both institutions merged some years later). If anywhere ought to have had successful SSFs, it was Hong Kong, where the market suffered from a series of inefficiencies such as:

- exchange-mandated bid–offer spreads you could drive a bus through (the minimum tick size was sometimes as much as 1% of the stock price);
- minimum commission of 50 basis points per round trip;
- stamp duty of 25 basis points per round trip;
- short-selling banned or severely restricted.

As Mark Beddis notes:

> A stock needed to move as much as 2% before you could even sniff a profit. In contrast, these stock futures seemed to represent the sweet smell of freedom for beleaguered traders. The SSF tick size was one basis point, there was no minimum commission and no stamp duty and you could short them all day if you wanted. How could they fail?

Remarkably, Hong Kong's SSFs did fail. The market remains essentially moribund to this day. Yet, on the Stock exchange spreads remain wide, and remarkably Hong Kong still maintains a minimum commission level, along with stamp duty (albeit much reduced from its 1994 levels). The reasons for Hong Kong's failure are intriguing, but we would tend to pin the blame on the initial reluctance to create specific market-makers to induce liquidity and indeed the cross-asset issue that has plagued various SSFs launches. In other words, the folk who had access to the cash rarely had access to the futures market, while the futures players could rarely access the cash market competitively (as they weren't stock exchange members). Precisely the same fate befell the Sydney Futures Exchange's attempt to launch SSFs shortly after Hong Kong. The SFE's membership, while frequently drawn from the same institutions, was often from disparate backgrounds—namely, money market and bonds at SFE and equities at the Australian Stock Exchange (ASX). The two groups rarely crossed over from their home exchanges. Therefore, there was no ability to make prices on futures against cash and vice versa, and one might argue that ultimately the whole market was the loser. Certainly, a key issue in the success of MEFF's SSFs in particular seems to have been their ability to bring all the cash and futures players together in one forum and thus create what can be argued was the world's first truly successful SSFs market.

Of course one key argument in relation to Hong Kong, or Sydney and any other unsuccessful exchange, remains the idea that there may just be no demand for the SSFs product. Certainly, the world's leading futures and options exchange, EUREX, has wholeheartedly championed this view. Once again the USA is going to truly provide the acid test in this respect:

> What is it about futures that make them so wonderful? A successful futures contract has one core defining characteristic: it meets a need that nothing else can satisfy quite as well. That need may vary from one market to another but is always there. In a single transaction, commodity producers can hedge their forward production for years ahead; portfolio managers can use index futures to alter their entire risk profile and money managers can smooth out their 10 year interest rate exposure using bond or interest rate futures. Until futures came along, there was just no quick way to substantially modify your risk profile in asset classes that were as complex as commodities, benchmarked equities and debt.
>
> Mark Beddis (2002)

So, what makes SSFs so advantageous? Well, in some ways, there is a degree of fallacious argument that futures need to make a remarkable difference to any market to be truly successful. For instance, in money markets, the OTC forward rate agreements and exchange-traded short-term interest rate futures are remarkably similar in many characteristics, but both markets thrive for their own specific reasons—each indeed helps feed the other, in a virtuous circle for liquidity. Exchange Traded Funds and Stock Index Futures achieve largely identical outcomes for traders, yet both can, thanks to their slight differences, thrive. Precisely the same is true of SSFs. Even without frustrating cash market impediments, such as the US "uptick" rule, SSFs are still at a great advantage for those wishing to sell a stock short, particularly one that may be tightly held or for some other reason be difficult to borrow stock in. In that respect, SSFs can help add liquidity to stocks and ensure they are more reasonably priced than may be possible with stocks that are very prone to being squeezed, due to a lack of stock supply for shorting.

If one argues that the main ingredients to successful futures markets have been efficient risk transfer, circumvention of market inefficiencies, and price discovery then one can see that in many respects futures can enhance the equity market, just as they enhanced the bond market. In many instances stock market spreads are quite woeful compared with their futures markets cousins (in the case of, say, bond or money market products). There is no reason that the interrelationship of SSFs and cash equities cannot help reduce the real costs of dealing (namely, the bid–offer spread), in a world where commissions have already been reduced to historically low levels with the prospects of technology further reducing these costs in forthcoming years.

True, the US stock market already has remarkable depth and liquidity for its largest stocks, but the fact remains that in many instances there is still greater flexibility of execution in the futures market, and block-trading facilities can further enhance the ability to move large blocks of futures between institutions. After all, if there was no need for single equity derivatives, why is there already such a thriving market for Equity Swaps and Contracts For Difference (CFDs)? When it comes to price discovery, there is a lot of discussion on how the US stock market actually discovers prices so accurately. Yet, the truth is the US equity market, while presenting a form of united front across the NYSE and NASDAQ, is in fact a hotchpotch of executing platforms, and, in the wake of all the public indignation surrounding the likes of analysts recommendations in recent years, it is remarkable that regulators continue to ignore the worst injustice served upon investors: the fact that their orders may often be exercised on an ECN or some other alternative platform far from the madding crowd of the stock exchange, quite feasibly at a disadvantageous price to the market elsewhere. Indeed, nobody can really say quite what the overall stock price is during a session, as trading is in so many disparate places. Likewise, the fact that in most SSFs environments a trader can enter an order that will be shown to the market, as opposed to the likes of the NYSE where his order is at the mercy of a monopolistic market-maker (or specialist), suggests that for all the volume in the US stock market it may yet require at least, let us say, a little fine-tuning to be regarded as a genuinely modern democratic marketplace. SSFs offer greater democracy and transparency than any existing cash platform.

In respect of margin requirements, even in the USA where margins of 20% have been applied (essentially more than twice the European average), this still compares very favourably with the US stock margin minimum of 50%. Similarly, when it comes to clearing and settlement, where the most advanced stock markets are largely struggling to get to grips with anything much below $T +$ several, the SSFs market already effectively offers real-time same day $(T + 0)$ clearing of futures transactions—although of course deliveries are slowed by the resulting speed of the cash market settlement process.

Of course, one key issue for SSFs proponents (which in our view has not been adequately prepared for at the time of writing) remains the fact that as soon as there is a major pullback (perhaps only a single day sharp fall), SSFs will bear the brunt of the blame for the collapse, as the pro-Uptick reactionaries blame the impact of futures. This is an eventuality that the SSF exchanges need to prepare themselves for, and it can be argued that, with their very lean structures, they are not adequately prepared to defeat an onslaught from what remains a Wall Street where many were weaned on cash equities and remain fairly disdainful of the many well-documented benefits of derivative products.

Equally, those who view futures as products that have enjoyed instant success on every one of their launches overlook many key aspects in the history of organized derivatives markets. Bond futures (initially based around GNMA[7] markets) proved sluggish at first. Likewise for various other products that have since become notably successful—such as Swap Futures, which have had various incarnations over the past decade, and in very recent years there have been significant breakthroughs such as the LIFFE Swapnote, which was a development of the similar, but less successful LIBOR[8] Financed Bond marketplace. In that respect, SSFs may yet need fine-tuning to really make headway. Indeed, the Euronext LIFFE market, for instance, may opt for more deliverable contracts, especially as the market's demand seemed to be heading in that direction at the time of writing, even though there was no discernible preference among potential end-users when LIFFE launched the product in January 2001.

We remain unconvinced over the claim that US markets have achieved perfection in risk transfer as espoused by many market observers. If specialists are doing such a perfect job, why do we have ECNs in the first place? Indeed, what happens with most markets in which there is a key exchange-listed derivative—the derivative often becomes the benchmark for pricing (in the same sort of backward way that we also employ Black–Scholes to give an options price by reintroducing something already in the mix)! In the USA, despite there having been a large scandal over analysts during 2002/2003, we're never sure exactly where the best execution is at any one point in time—but can anybody be certain for that matter? The reason may be the exchange or it could easily be any of a clutch of ECNs. Having said that, people ought to be free to execute what they want where they want. However, an SSF will, by its flexibility to be arbitraged, create a coherent single price focus, just as T-Bond futures do for US government securities, etc.

Nevertheless, the argument about SSFs is not about to be settled. Although, as volume grows, particularly Euronext LIFFE and MEFF push the argument forward bit by bit every day. With the new US exchanges onstream, it will still take a product development cycle of perhaps 12 to 18 months from their late November (2002) launch to see a coherent volume level, which can be regarded as a benchmark to test the success of the marketplace. The sheer cost of launching such a vast new product area is undoubtedly what has induced the primary US SSFs players to enter partnerships (LIFFE with NASDAQ, the OneChicago market uniting the futures and options exchanges of the Windy

---

[7] GNMA—the Government National Mortgage Association—is known as "Ginnie Mae" and is a US-government-owned agency that buys mortgages from institutions and then sells them in a securitized form to investors as bonds.

[8] LIBOR—London Inter Bank Offer Rate—in other words the minimum wholesale lending rate of banks in London. LIBOR is often a benchmark for many international lending rates.

City) and therefore indulge themselves in a little risk transfer of their own devising.

As previously discussed, SSFs date from the 17th century when they were used on the Amsterdam exchange in Holland. They then experienced an extended hibernation period, with their listing in Sweden, then Hong Kong, Australia, and then South Africa (among others) marking their reintroduction a number of years ago. As one of the longest standing advocates of their reintroduction in Europe and the US, it was of course a delight for Patrick Young, co-author of this book, to see LIFFE undertaking their substantial USF initiative in late 2000—a launch with which he remains delighted to have been associated.

True, SSFs face some very tough competition in certain jurisdictions. Perhaps most notably in the UK, the market has strong opposition from spread-betting companies (offering a form of gambling that is really trading, but cleverly exploits UK gambling laws) and CFDs, an OTC marketplace for a sort of perpetual stock future (see below) that is used by private investors and institutions alike. As spread bets and CFDs are both functions of cash-dealing, one can argue there is superior liquidity at the time of writing in the London market compared with the Euronext LIFFE exchange, for instance, but then again the central counterparty clearing of SSFs is a key issue in helping to make the exchange-traded product somewhat safer in terms of overall credit risk.

Compared with CFDs and similar products, the whole SSFs position of a price encompassing everything is much easier for the end-user to follow. There is inherent simplicity in the whole concept of just buying or selling an instrument with initial margin and mark-to-market/variation margin as opposed to a position that basically costs something for every day you seek to hold it. It's not merely the bureaucracy, it's an all-encompassing capital efficiency issue. The reason LIFFE's USFs were a revolution in equities-trading was because they finally brought us a cheap, simple, and efficient method of trading international equities, which had previously been absent in the marketplace. Of course, it's difficult for the CFD houses to come to terms with such commoditized dealing, as they already make a much better percentage from the whole trading process compared with the mere nickels that an exchange such as LIFFE or NQLX receives for providing the entire connect-dealing business for its products.

Clearing remains the key issue that stands out when comparing SSFs with their OTC brethren. When you deal with a CFD agency, you are utilizing a market-maker who demands a price (allowing himself a stage in the process— thus adding to your hidden costs). The fact that this market-maker then knows your position when you return to exit is a secondary, but also highly significant issue—where true dealing costs are concerned. True, many CFD traders argue this is irrelevant, but with SSFs the problem of anybody being able to recall your position as in large cosmopolitan markets does not arise: it is simply not possible. The question to ask yourself is: Would you really sleep easily at night if your money was left with a single counterparty to whom you have no recourse in the event of a financial crisis?

The Enron collapse wreaked havoc with many folk—such as ship-forwarders—whose hedges became worthless overnight. With CFD brokers who use a third party market-maker: What happens to your position if the market-maker closes down? When you deal on a recognized exchange—be it OneChicago, MEFF, or whoever—your position and money are truly ring-fenced at the most secure financial institution known to man: the clearing house (e.g., the London Clearing House [LCH] for LIFFE). In a world where a titan such as Enron can go bankrupt, there is simply no CFD company with a balance sheet for its CFD dealing operation that can compete with the safety of the LCH.

Overall, there is simply no reason to believe that a risk transfer mechanism should be based on individual equities any more than it can be based on indices, individual commodities, bond markets, or energy products. Indeed, some individual multinational stocks are arguably already larger than many existing markets on which commodity futures have been based.

COMPETING PRODUCTS

There are a number of competing and contiguous products alongside SSFs, which are worth examining.

Options

The original argument of many in the options trading community was that SSFs could be created synthetically by a combination of calls and puts. This was a very fair assertion, and we will examine synthetic trades in the trading section. However, the basic economics of the situation are not in favour of the end-user. To create an options position with two legs, the bid–offer spread can be greater than that for a single options leg, and, equally, the investor will usually end up paying more than a single brokerage charge. True, options spreads as a trade often have narrower bid–offer spreads than two outright options priced individually; but, even then, they are usually larger than a single futures contract. Equally, there are often spread brokerage concessions for multi-legged strategies, but a single futures commission is still invariably cheaper.

Warrants

The warrant market provides many opportunities for traders and once again synthetic stock futures can be created, although the issue of paying double-brokerage and an extended bid–offer spread makes the concept relatively uneconomic compared with simply buying a single SSF.

CFDs

Contracts for Difference provide a very close competitive threat to SSFs, although they are a somewhat different product from highly commoditized exchange-traded SSFs.

A CFD is an OTC derivative product that has become popular in the UK for two main reasons:

- it offers leverage in equity investments (margin-trading of ordinary equities is uncommon in the UK);
- it offers an opportunity to short the market that can be more easily administered than selling stock short.

The CFD involves a series of parameters. Essentially, the investor takes on a contract to either buy or sell shares in a framework that may be described as a perpetual or open-ended futures position. You may specify a settlement date on entering a position, although this is relatively uncommon. Obviously, the potentially perpetual nature of a CFD can be very useful for a longer term holder of the position, as there is no need to roll over positions as is the case when futures contracts expire. However, CFDs also require the investor to make specific payments during the period they hold their positions. For instance, from the moment purchasers of a CFD open up a position, they are effectively paying a charge for the leverage implied in their position. Therefore, a position of say X dollars, at an interest rate of $Y\%$, will attract a daily carry charge of Z dollars for every day the position is held. Generally speaking, financing charges for long positions are around 2.5–3% over LIBOR in the UK market. For short positions, the seller of a CFD usually receives interest at around LIBOR minus 2.5–3%, again calculated on a daily basis.

Similarly, dividend payments do not accrue as they would with a cash equity transaction. Although no dividends are payable to SSF holders, this is however factored into the price of the SSF. For long CFD positions, around 80–90% of the dividend is usually received by the holder, while short-sellers must pay the full dividend amount.

As CFDs trade OTC and not through an exchange, the issue of best price is always important. Usually, market-makers will set a price close to the stock market levels prevailing, although investors need to be careful to monitor what this is and indeed may have limited recourse against a CFD broker, even if they discover their CFD price is not close to the prevailing market level. CFDs are usually packaged by a specialist market-maker, although the position is administered through a broker—which means traders lack the security of a clearing house.

We believe that for the most liquid, largest traded equities, SSFs will invariably prove the best available option for those seeking leverage of the many other benefits of derivatives trade. When you are keen to seek a position in a liquid, but perhaps not quite absolutely top-flight stock, then CFDs make an ideal instrument. The one key issue to recall with regard to CFDs is that the introduction of SSFs basically grows the pool for equity derivatives. CFDs will remain a key facet of derivatives-trading for the foreseeable future, but we believe they will be a niche marketplace for the tiers below the absolute top-grade stocks, which will increasingly be catered for with SSFs.

The liquidity and prices for SSFs and for CFDs both inherently relate to the underlying equity. However, whereas a CFD company's internal market-maker needs to make a turn in addition to the basic price, with the most organized exchanges the impressively thin spreads commonly seen on the SSFs are all you need to pay.

Likewise, commissions at somewhere around 0.25% of the whole amount of the geared CFD tend to be significantly higher than the commoditized prices of futures brokers who charge a single price for dealing. Of course, that's before calculating all the fiddly (and potentially costly) carry charges associated with the CFD position. Dividends alone can cost 100 per cent of the charge for a short CFD position, and the long end may only receive 80% of the same payment.

Overall, CFDs offer a strong alternative to SSFs, although as SSFs gain liquidity we believe that the CFD marketplace will retain its popularity, as of course any listed share can form the basis of a CFD. Therefore, it is quite plausible that the CFD business will continue to expand as a conduit for traders looking at stocks beyond the leading issues traded on exchange. Nevertheless, the danger for SSF markets remains the problem posed by high margins within some regulatory environments, while CFD markets tend to have a basic initial margin around 10–20% for retail investors. For wholesale investors, such as hedge funds, margin levels can be much lower with rates apparently as low as a few percent. This of course provides a significant competitive advantage for CFDs.

CFDs are gradually becoming available in many European and some Asian markets, although US regulators have not yet allowed them to be made available for US investors.

Spread-betting

Spread-betting is another UK innovation that, like CFDs, are gradually being offered in other countries (although not the USA). Spread-betting in single shares is usually based on quarterly, futures-style contracts, although the bookmakers also provide weekly share markets. Spread-betting companies also tend to make markets in leading initial public offering issues on a when issued basis ahead of their official listing on stock markets.

Spread-betting usually involves a larger bid–offer spread than in cash or conventional futures markets, because it is on this spread that bookmakers make their profits. Initial margins tend to be around 10–20%. Similarly, investors need to realize that their positions are held by a bookmaker and not by a clearing house, presenting a modicum of credit risk. When it comes to closing the position out, the holder is at the mercy of the price made by the bookmaker, although this ought to be proximate to the share price, as otherwise arbitrage would be possible. Nevertheless, the bid–offer spread may be a cause for concern, although recent spread-betting advertising for various companies has argued to the contrary.

Equity swaps

Equity swaps are very similar in concept to currency or interest rate swaps. They are contractual agreements involving two counterparties, providing for periodic exchange of cash flows during a specified time period. In the case of equity swaps, at least one of the two payment flows is linked to the returns on a basket of shares, an equity index, or even a single stock. A plain vanilla or standard equity swap involves one counterparty agreeing to pay the other the total returns from an equity index in return for the total return from some other asset, which may, for example be, an interest rate. The payments are all based on a fixed notional amount covering a predetermined, fixed time period. Overall, equity swap structures are highly flexible and are frequently created with maturities ranging from a few months through to 10 years. Swaps provide a useful vehicle to exchange the returns on one asset for the returns of another without the problem of incurring the transaction costs typical in the cash market (this is especially relevant for large equity swaps where the underlying stock market would have difficulty absorbing large blocks of cash equity). Therefore, equity swaps are a very useful investment vehicle and asset allocation tool. Swaps are inherently flexible and their payment terms can be denominated in any currency regardless of the underlying equities/equity index involved, and payments can be exchanged monthly, quarterly, annually, or even at maturity as a balloon payment.

There is an ostensibly infinite number of variations on the plain vanilla equity swap theme, which include, but are not remotely limited to:

- international equity swaps where the equity return is linked to an international equity index;
- currency-hedged swaps where the swap is structured to eliminate currency risk;

- call swaps, where the equity payment component is not paid unless the equity index/basket/individual share appreciates in value. If the value of the equity component depreciates or fails to meet a pre-specified benchmark return, then there will be no payment to the counterparty receiving the equity return, due to the protection afforded by the call component.

With specific regard to SSFs, an equity swap could take place where one counterparty pays a fixed capital amount of dollar-denominated LIBOR, while receiving the total return on a specific US equity on a quarterly basis (e.g., Microsoft). The swaps' advantages include the lack of transaction costs, no withholding taxes on dividends et al., and no tracking error or basis risk issue with regard to actually trying to buy the cash equity itself.

Overall, each product has its own merits and time will ultimately prove that CFDs, for instance, have a very healthy niche, although the concentrated, commoditized liquidity within the more cost-effective USFs means they will invariably become the more significant asset class—particularly among retail investors. In essence, the CFD niche will enjoy very healthy growth for many years to come throughout the world. The stock futures market is still truly pre-adolescent in its growth, but, as the US gathers pace, it will continue to build on its significant progress to date.

3
Trading Single Stock Futures

The opportunities for trading Single Stock Futures (SSFs) are considerable. Naturally, the simplest trades involve simply buying and selling SSF contracts. Once again, experienced traders who may find it a total bore to read such elementary information may prefer to skip a page or two ...

For investors who wish to exploit strategies that involve more than merely mono-dimensionally hanging on to existing shares, SSFs provide a simple means to trade on the many vagaries of market movements, and we will address some of these strategies later in this chapter.

ELECTRONIC FUTURES—A NEW PARADIGM FOR THE USA

Especially for traders in the USA, SSFs provide a unique new dimension to trading—namely, the electronic marketplace. Whereas traditionally US futures markets have involved intermediating via the pits to gain a price fill, now traders anywhere can log on and see their orders being listed on the screen with Time Price Order priority. This first-in-first-out order entry system allows traders to have the opportunity to trade with each other and hopefully help keep spreads at their narrowest possible levels. It provides a rich opportunity for any trader to enter the market on the same terms as everybody else. Similarly, the price you see on the screen is at least the price currently trading—whereas even the best data vendors are often a fraction behind the actual pit prices. In this respect, the directness of access to pretty much all of the world's SSFs makes them an intriguing product group. Coupled with the directness of access to options markets such as the International Securities Exchange and the Boston Options Exchange, the prospects for direct, more democratic electronic access to US markets in particular have never looked brighter. Compared with the rather archaic specialist system on the NYSE, the possibility of electronic trading directly to a market like NASDAQ LIFFE is a most interesting one.

CAVEAT: WHEN IS A TRADING DAY NOT A TRADING DAY

Before traders enter a market, they need to know when, in the international world of SSFs, every stock is trading. If there is no underlying cash market trading, then individual equity derivatives (futures and options) will not be open to trade on any derivatives exchange, even if that market *is* open. This means that, for instance, although the Euronext LIFFE exchange is open on December 24th and 31st, various Universal Stock Futures (USFs) do not trade. Tables 3.1 and 3.2 show which markets were open in LIFFE's USF portfolio (we use LIFFE as it remains the broadest international market of all for SSFs—in fact, most SSFs markets are essentially domestic, even in the USA). The Euronext LIFFE exchange opens from 08:00–12:30 on both these days, hence the earlier than usual close in some markets.

Above all else, traders need to keep a very close eye on just when their SSFs are going to trade. Although national holidays across Europe are roughly co-ordinated on some major ecclesiastical (e.g., Christmas, Easter) or political dates (e.g., May Day), there is a multiplicity of local holidays, which can

Table 3.1 Trading hours for USF contracts
Tuesday, December 24th, 2002

Country of origin	Future/Option	Open (hours)	Pre-close	Close (hours)
Denmark	F	Closed	Closed	Closed
Finland	F	Closed	Closed	Closed
France	**F**	**08:00**	**12:28**	**12:30**
Germany	F	Closed	Closed	Closed
Ireland	F	Closed	Closed	Closed
Italy	F	Closed	Closed	Closed
Netherlands	**F**	**08:00**	**12:28**	**12:30**
Norway	F	Closed	Closed	Closed
Spain	F	Closed	Closed	Closed
Sweden	F	Closed	Closed	Closed
Switzerland	F	Closed	Closed	Closed
UK	**F**	**08:00**	**12:28**	**12:30**
USA	**F**	**08:00**	**12:28**	**12:30**

Table 3.2 Trading hours for USF contracts
Tuesday, December 31st, 2002

Country of origin	Future/Option	Open (hours)	Pre-close	Close (hours)
Denmark	F	Closed	Closed	Closed
Finland	F	Closed	Closed	Closed
France	**F**	**08:00**	**12:28**	**12:30**
Germany	F	Closed	Closed	Closed
Ireland	**F**	**08:00**	**12:28**	**12:30**
Italy	F	Closed	Closed	Closed
Netherlands	**F**	**08:00**	**12:28**	**12:30**
Norway	F	Closed	Closed	Closed
Spain	F	Closed	Closed	Closed
Sweden	F	Closed	Closed	Closed
Switzerland	F	Closed	Closed	Closed
UK	**F**	**08:00**	**12:28**	**12:30**
USA	**F**	**08:00**	**12:28**	**12:30**

result in traders finding themselves expecting activity in a particular stock on a certain day when, in fact, due to local holidays, that market is closed to derivatives-trading.

Okay, so let's start looking at some simple strategies and build up to the slightly more complex stuff as this chapter progresses. The only thing we can be utterly certain about is that this list will never be remotely comprehensive. As the SSFs market grows, more and more intriguing uses of the product are going to be defined, and, indeed, even as we write, there remains the very strong possibility that some unique strategies employing a mix of many products (including, but not limited to, individual stock futures and options, index products, and exchange-traded funds) are already being deployed by the most advanced traders in this marketplace.

The same health warnings apply to this chapter as the last one—more advanced traders may prefer to skip the very simple stuff at the start of the chapter.

PROFITING FROM A SHARE PRICE RISE

Obviously, one can simply buy a share and wait for it to rise. However, especially in the short term, it is more cash-efficient to exploit margin and use an SSF to achieve the same position. True, no dividend is paid to an SSF holder, but this is already factored into the price of the SSF. Also, UK investors benefit from the lack of stamp duty on SSFs. Another advantage is that futures contracts tend to be cheaper to execute as bid–offer spreads and commissions are frequently narrower and lower, respectively.

Take a stock such as Microsoft (regularly the most traded stock in the initial weeks of business on the US SSFs markets). Let's hypothesize on a simple long trade.

On December 6th, the share price of Microsoft was 55.55 and the February future was trading at 55.61. By January 17th, the stock reaches a price of 57.25 and the February futures are trading at 57.28.

Obviously, in this example, we can see that both the underlying share price and the futures price have risen. Of course, the gains are largely the same, overall:

$$\text{Stock} \quad 57.25 - 55.55 = 170$$
$$\text{Futures} \quad 57.28 - 55.61 = 167$$

As the futures premium has slightly reduced during this time, the cash equity made a slightly greater gain of 170 ticks compared with 167 ticks for the futures. However, in terms of total return related to the outlay, the story is very different.

Buying the stock at full price would cost $5,555 for 100 shares. A single 100-share contract of SSFs at 20% initial margin would cost $1,112.2 upfront.

The total return therefore is vastly greater on the SSF in relation to the overall amount of the investment, thanks to the margin-gearing effect—even in the USA, where margins are commensurately much higher than in most other SSFs markets.

Overall, the cash position makes $170 while the futures position, thanks to the slight narrowing of the premium, makes a profit of $167. On the other hand, against a purchase cost of $5,555, the return on the stock is a healthy 3.6%. However, even with US margins, the return on the $1,112.2 initial margin is a much superior 15% return.

PROFITING FROM A SHARE PRICE FALL

Of course, a key advantage to using SSFs is their ability to allow traders to easily sell a market short. Moreover, the US uptick rule enforced on cash equities does not apply to selling SSFs. Selling cash stock short can often be an administratively tricky procedure with added costs and bureaucracy for the trader (presuming they even can sell stock short—often a difficult process for retail investors), but is not an issue with SSFs.

In another case an investor believes the price of Microsoft shares is going to fall. The cash stock market is at 55.55 and the February Futures are at 55.61. By January 17th, in this hypothetical example, the stock has fallen to 54.00 and the February SSF has fallen to 54.03:

$$Stock \quad 55.55 - 54.00 = 155$$
$$Futures \quad 55.61 - 54.03 = 158$$

In this case, note how the stock has fallen by slightly less than the future, as the futures premium to the cash has again reduced itself to just three ticks. So, here we have a win–win situation, a larger profit ($158 against $155) for the futures over the cash and a much greater percentage return, thanks to the leverage of margin. In fact, the cash position makes a net profit (presuming a 50% margin on shorting stock—$2,777.50) of 5.69%, while the future with 20% margin (again $1,112.2) returns a percentage gain of 14.2%.

Remember, neither party gets to use the cash from the sold position in cash or SSFs markets, and this margin is an extra charge on top of withholding the margin by the clearing house or clearing broker in the case of the cash stock.

A HEALTH WARNING

Okay, so it's all well and good to look at hypothetical examples when they work to your advantage, but right now a sound health warning is required for all aspiring SSFs traders.

In the first example we highlighted just how cash-efficient SSFs can be, even with the relatively high US margins of 20%. Well, that's absolutely true when things are going your way, but always, always, always remember that gearing is a two-way street and once you let it get the better of you it can carry you out faster than you can say LTCM![1]

The most vital thing to learn in futures-trading is that you are going to be wrong and, more than likely, more often wrong than right. With futures, you are not going to suddenly turn short-term speculations in to long-term trades with any great ease. Rather, you need to get into the habit of good traders and bear in mind that you must enter every trade with a very finite idea of where your exit point for a trade lies if it goes wrong. Employ stop orders at every possible juncture, for without them you will surely perish on the funeral pyre of burned out futures traders, which grows larger with every day as a seemingly endless stream of traders ignore the risks and pay attention only to the possible

---

[1] LTCM—or Long-Term Credit Management—had various Nobel laureates create essentially perfect algorithms for trading financial markets. Alas, the real world is less perfect than they realized and the resulting hedge fund's collapse caused ripples through the New York and global financial community.

upside. Ignore the profit potential would be our suggestion and pay attention to not losing money—and where you must lose money, lose as little as you can. Never ever let your losses grow beyond the level you set initially and always set that level pragmatically (e.g., just below notable support on the charts for long positions). Anyway, doubtless you already know all about stops and deploying them to ensure your financial safety, but we can't avoid giving you this financial health warning even though you may have heard it a thousand times before. In fact, there's a very good reason that you have heard it a thousand times before ... it's an absolutely vital process to follow!

"PAIRS" (RELATIVE VALUE) TRADING

As we mentioned earlier, traditionally, selling shares short has been difficult and has precluded many investors from partaking of one of the more common professional tools: pairs-trading. However, even institutional investors can find pairs-trading with SSFs a more efficient use of their capital and a less bureaucratic means of selling and administering the short leg of the position.

Pairs-trading simply involves having a reasonably agnostic viewpoint on market direction, but feeling convinced that a particular relationship in the price between two different companies is going to expand or contract. With stock futures, the whole issue of borrowing stock or having dividend liability while short of a cash share is essentially reduced. Margin payments are the only ongoing position maintenance you need to make with SSFs, and, in fact, margins are reduced for the relatively lesser risk of spread positions such as pairs trades.

Pairs-trading is also, of course, the basis of the original hedge fund concept of maintaining a short position against every long position (aka the "hedge"). Pairs trades can be undertaken for a multiplicity of reasons, such as one company being expected to pay a higher dividend than another through likely management differences or perceived relative strength/weakness on technical bases (whether through charts or some other analysis method).

Normally, pairs trades take place between two stocks in a similar sector. Where SSF pairs are transacted on the same exchange, there is usually a significant margin reduction as pairs trades have less overall risk exposure. Also, note that on various exchanges (such as Euronext LIFFE), electronic matching technology allows pairs trades to be executed as a strategy trade with both legs being transacted simultaneously, thus reducing execution risks (e.g., slippage) to the trader.

During 2001 the oil sector was particularly volatile. For many weeks both BP and Shell were trading at or around the same price. On July 30th, the December Shell share futures could be sold at 594 pence, while BP could be bought for 584 pence. In other words, BP was 10 pence cheaper than Shell (i.e., a spread level of -10), and in this trade we were expecting BP to outperform Shell stock, relatively, prior to the expiry of the December futures. The LIFFE USFs were the ideal vehicle here.

The mid-September oil price spike in the wake of 09/11, added to an already volatile market, gave the spread extra oomph and indeed on September 21st it was as wide as 85 points for a while. Note that this is $+85$ points, a difference of some 95 points from where we entered the trade. Of course, it is often only with hindsight that such a trade could have been exited so perfectly ... However, the profit levels of the position were rarely an issue. For most of October 2001, the differential sat at around 50 points, which meant a healthy 60 point profit for the trade, given that we originally bought BP cheaper than we sold Shell, and at this time we could buy the Shell position back much more cheaply than we could sell the BP trade.

Note that during this period, both shares went ex-dividend for their interim payments on August 15. At gross rates of 6.5 pence for Shell and 4.3 pence for BP, there was little change in their prices. While SSFs (like equity options) are priced to reflect the dividend payments, no actual dividend payments change hands in the SSFs market, further simplifying the issue for the spread (or outright) trader.

Essentially, if you get pairs trades right then you can profit enormously, if you get it wrong the fact that you are holding two legs to the trade ought to help cushion any losses, compared with being wrong in an outright position.

RELATIVE MARKET PERFORMANCE

Once again the flexible nature of SSFs and indeed index futures allows us the luxury of trading a single (or indeed multiple SSFs) relative to a narrow sectoral or broad market index.

TAX EFFICIENCY TRADES

There are many ways to exploit derivatives in a quest for greater tax efficiency, as frequently taxation rules differ between different jurisdictions and even within jurisdictions they can be different for different types of product. Income and capital gains tax treatments usually differ, as do taxes levied on domestic or overseas investors. In this section, we seek to illustrate some core, basic principles. We do not intend to provide detailed tax advice, so readers should not believe they are armed with the minutiae of their own tax regime after reading this section! Given that this book is being distributed in a number of countries on several continents, we baulk at being held accountable for the separate tax policies of a host of different nations. Nevertheless, some basic principles can be discerned from a few examples:

Dividend taxes

It is often the case that dividends attract a higher rate of taxation for foreign investors. Of course, in the case of SSFs, no dividends are payable. Rather the dividend itself is priced into the future. This leads to an interesting situation where there is a different taxation regime for domestic and overseas investors, as this leads to the two different investor groups imputing different fair value prices in the futures market:

• domestic investors (who receive higher net dividends) will impute a lower fair value futures price;
• overseas investors (who receive a lower net dividend) will impute a higher fair value futures price.

Intriguingly, the actual market price of an SSF can often be somewhere in-between these two prices, permitting both sets of stock holders the opportunity to make an arbitrage (i.e., risk-free) profit from their underlying long positions. Domestic investors who own the shares and receive the dividend at the lower tax rate have the opportunity to sell futures at what is for them an artificially high price. Meanwhile, foreign investors holding the stock who pay a higher rate of tax and therefore receive a lower net dividend can buy the futures in the anticipation that the market is actually undervalued relative to their dividend position.

Take the following example. In France, domestic investors receive a tax credit of 15% along with their dividends. Non-domestic investors do not receive the same credit. BNP Paribas announces a dividend of 2.20 euros per share. Therefore, with a 15% tax credit added on, the domestic French investor will receive €2.53, while the overseas investors will receive only €2.20. The market price of the underlying share is currently:

BNP Paribas share   Bid   80.00   Offer   80.02

In this case, the French investor has a fair value share price for BNP of €78.27 per share (i.e., 80.01 + 0.79 interest cost −2.53 dividend). Meanwhile, the non-French investor has a higher fair value at €78.60 (80.01 + 0.79 interest cost − 2.20 dividend). So, the fair value figures are:

Domestic investor   78.27

Overseas investor   78.60

However, the market price of the future lies between the two fair value figures:

BNP Paribas future   Bid 78.40   Offer 78.44

Therefore, each investor group (domestic and overseas) can enhance their investment returns using SSFs. An overseas investor can sell the underlying

BNP Paribas shares and buy BNP Paribas futures. The money received on the sale of the shares can also be placed on deposit to earn interest. After the dividend has been paid, the prices are as follows:

	Bid	Offer
BNP Paribas share	82.00	82.02
BNP Paribas futures	82.32	82.36

The shares in this instance have still risen during this period despite the dividend being paid. For the non-domestic investor, the gain would be €1.98 per share plus the dividend of 2.20 (i.e., a 5.2% return on the original share price). The return from the futures strategy, which pays no dividend, would be 3.88 per share, which added to an interest income (equivalent to 0.47 cents per share) gives a 5.5% return on the original share price. The position can then be switched back into long shares to maintain the long investment position, although exposure to long futures means that any capital gains exposure to BNP Paribas shares has been maintained.

A domestic investor can also profit in this scenario by selling futures at the relatively high price of 78.40, while at the same time buying shares. This of course establishes a risk-neutral position with regard to BNP Paribas's share price. After payment of the dividend, the shareholding would yield a return of 1.98 plus the dividend of 2.53 per share. The futures position would have produced a loss of 3.96, resulting in a net return of 0.55 per share. Of course, interest costs of 0.47 would be payable, but then again a risk-free return of 0.06 per share can be a welcome fillip to many investment portfolios!

Of course brokerage is not included in these examples, so overall returns would be lower, but, nonetheless, the point remains valid that both domestic and non-domestic investors can often profit from a difference in dividend taxation!

Some issues on income versus capital gains

Different types of investment funds and private investors will have various ways of maximizing their gains, as their taxation treatment may be preferable as either capital gains or income tax. Once again this is a highly complex issue and professional accounting advice for your situation and jurisdiction should be sought. However, to illustrate some key principals, we will display some theoretical examples later in this section. Overall, the key issue to recall is that SSFs can permit an investor to shift the balance of their portfolio between capital gains and income, while also widening the pool of instruments the investor can have recourse to.

As already mentioned, futures contracts do not pay dividends. Therefore an investment in futures can be employed as an alternative to investing in high-yield shares. By holding an equivalent cash balance on deposit to the value of the underlying shares that could be purchased, you can garner the same total return as would be the case with an underlying share position. In other words, you are not geared to this position. If you don't maintain the full cash deposit, then you have a position that garners less interest income, but more significantly is more leveraged to any underlying price movement.

For example, let's look at a simple dividend switch play. Let us assume that AstraZeneca are due to pay a dividend of 35 pence per share. By switching an underlying equity position into futures, we can reduce the income earned on the investment, but without any impact on our exposure to the stock or the return on our investment:

	Bid	Offer
Share	3200p	3205p
Future	3202p	3212p

The shares are sold at 3200p, and the cash received from the sale is deposited to earn interest. An equivalent number of SSFs are purchased at 3212p.

Once the shares go ex-dividend, the market prices are as follows:

	Bid	Offer
Share	3150p	3155p
Future	3185p	3195p

So, over the period, holding shares would have resulted in a capital loss of 55 pence with a dividend income of 35 pence to make a net loss of 20 pence. Holding futures would have resulted in a capital loss of 27 pence (i.e., 3212p − 3185p) and an interest income of 7 pence, again a net loss of 20 pence per share. So, the use of futures has here reduced the amount of income accrued by the fund without in any way changing the overall return (brokerage costs accepted admittedly).

Therefore, portfolio income can be minimized by switching stock positions into futures positions ahead of an ex-dividend date and then switching back into the stock after the stock has gone ex-dividend. Total investment return is unaffected, but dividend income is eliminated, while there is minimal interest income. Total share price exposure is maintained throughout the position.

Increasing portfolio income

Naturally, the same approach can also be deployed to increase portfolio income (e.g., for an investor who wishes to reduce capital gains exposure). Instead of buying shares that pay no dividends, depositing cash and buying futures contracts will generate an interest income and therefore a commensurately lower capital gain. Nevertheless, once again the total return will be the same as that generated from holding the shares, because SSFs ensure that exposure to share price movements is maintained.

For example, Intel pays no dividend. Judicious use of futures contracts can generate some interest income, while maintaining the same overall return as the share itself:

Share   18.87

Future   18.80

Let's compare the strategy of buying the share for three months and the notion of buying a three-month future and depositing the cash. After three months we can either trade out of the SSF or we may take it to settlement if it is a cash-settled contract (a deliverable contract would oblige us to buy the underlying equity, which may be something we ultimately want to do, but we'll presume not for this example—remember, some exchanges have deliverable contracts and some have cash-settled markets).

After three months, the shares are still worth 18.87, making a gain/loss of zero. Had they moved, this would have been entirely a capital gain/loss. The futures have narrowed their premium, because time to expiry has grown closer and therefore standing at 18.85 they have actually netted us a tiny profit of five ticks, or $5 per 100-share contract. However, the money spent to purchase the cash shares was some $1,880. Allowing for a high margin of 20%, the margin was $386 leaving us with $1,880−$386 = $1,504 to invest.

So presuming we invest this at even a low annual rate of 2% per annum, the return on this money over three months is 7.52, a cash return of some 0.5% per share—not unhelpful even at a time of very low interest rates!

Therefore, by using futures, we have the same return as investing in the underlying shares (in this case, remarkably, a slightly better return, thanks to the premium movement!), but with an added element of interest income in the portfolio.

Capital gains tax—A UK example

In some respects a peculiarity of the UK market, many investors seek to book their tax gains or losses in a specific year, and in this respect SSFs can be exploited to allow investors to maintain their exposure to a stock even when they have to temporarily sell it at the end of one tax year before buying it back again early in the new tax year. Tax liabilities are calculated annually in the UK: at the end of a tax year, which runs to April 5th. Individuals have a free allowance for capital gains every year and are allowed to net out losses and profits. Once upon a time, a process of selling overnight and buying back the next day (in essence a sort of stock repo) was common late in the tax year and was known as "bed and breakfasting" (after English guest house institutions, which are not quite hotels). However, nowadays penalties apply if the investor reinvests in the same stock within 30 days of his original sale, in an effort to discourage the "bed and breakfast" transactions. However, SSFs are very useful in this regard as they enable an investor to sell his stock, while simultaneously buying an SSF to maintain the same exposure. In the UK, the LIFFE Basis Trading Facility allows the trade to take place simultaneously, which makes the transaction more efficient. At the end of the 30-day period the UK investor can sell the SSF position once again and buy back the stock to revert to the original position. Note that this form of transaction can be effected for two reasons:

- to crystallize a gain (usually to utilize an annual capital gains tax [CGT] allowance);
- to take a loss and therefore offset CGT arising on gains elsewhere.

Probably the hardy perennial of many British investors stock portfolios in recent decades has been British Telecom. Alas, in the wake of the telecoms meltdown at the end of the dotcom bubble in 2000, its prospects were dimmed somewhat, and the share demonstrated a remarkable ability to head south, in common, it might be added, with a plethora of other telecom stocks.

Meanwhile, the tax authorities have created rules to try and preclude investors indulging in the practice of "bed and breakfasting" to book either profits or losses in a particular tax year by means of selling a share at close of business and then buying it back the following morning. At present, the UK rules, for instance, preclude a loss or gain being booked for tax reasons where the investor re-enters the same equity within 30 days of exiting it.

However, SSFs (in this case, LIFFE's USFs) permitted a seamless way to ensure that users can always maintain exposure to a particular equity. Therefore, in the case of British Telecom, an investor has endured a very tough 18 months holding the stock through almost relentless losses. However, the prospect of selling out and not being exposed to the stock is hardly attractive, because the volatility in telecom shares as all sorts of events (such as 3G[2] licence goalposts being altered retrospectively) along with the underlying nature of the telco marketplace, means that share prices could rebound very rapidly.

Therefore, in mid-October 2001, had investors sought to sell out to realize a loss on a stock that had traded from over £12 to almost £3, they could have simply sold the stock and simultaneously bought a LIFFE USF at the same market price. True, forward pricing of the future may have caused a slight

---

[2] As any stock market observer will recall the 3G or Third Generation Internet licensing affair became somewhat of a farrago saddling telcos with debt just before the Telecoms, Media and Technology (TMT) marketplace collapsed.

discrepancy, but it would be a matter of a few pence. The only disadvantage to be suffered by investors would be that they would not receive any dividends through holding the stock future; but, it would be easier to do the transaction during a 30-day window when no such payment was pending.

Moreover, the LIFFE USF also covered the demerger into the "new" BT Group and BT mmO$_2$, because the stock future was split when the shares themselves split. (We will examine this particular transaction on p. 62 along with other issues concerning changes to already trading contracts).

CURRENCY EXPOSURE

When LIFFE launched the first basket of international SSFs in early 2001, they soon represented eleven different national markets and some five separate currencies (and indeed as their product range has expanded so too has the number of countries grown—nowadays Euronext LIFFE have contracts on shares in some seven different currencies: euros, Danish krone, Norwegian krone, Swiss francs, Swedish krona, sterling and US dollars). Of course, investors can buy overseas equities and then utilize currency forwards or futures to hedge any potential losses in the currency. However, a simpler approach may be to buy SSFs instead of the underlying equity, as the margin requirements mean that less capital needs to be converted into the other currency.

Initial margin is set in the currency of the contract itself. However, most clearing houses accept multi-currency deposits and collateral against margin liabilities. For example, the London Clearing House would permit a US margin liability to be covered by a UK Treasury Bill denominated in pounds sterling (or indeed a European government bill denominated in euros, etc.). For a sterling-based investor, in this instance the currency exposure is effectively zero—changes in the foreign exchange rate merely affect the return on capital, they have no impact on the value of the capital itself.

Take, for example, a European fund manager whose positions are denominated in euros buying a US stock like AOL Time Warner:

	Bid	Offer
Stock	$40.20	$40.22
Future	$40.60	$40.65

The fund manager invests $500,000 in AOL Time Warner stock and his margin is $6 per share at a price of $40.22. At this time the euro is trading at €1.10 per $1. A month later the share and future prices are as follows:

	Bid	Offer
Stock	$41.20	$41.22
Future	$41.45	$41.50

During this time the dollar has fallen by 4.5% against the euro. So now each $1 is worth €1.05. In dollar terms the shares have risen 2.4%, but because of the currency movement the shares have fallen 2.2% in euro terms. Had the fund manager bought the shares and invested the full value in euros, he would have a loss when he converted his funds back to euros even though the shares had actually risen in price!

However, by exploiting SSFs, only the initial margin of €81,840 was converted into US dollars. The value of this initial margin in US dollars is now €78,120. The fund manager has made a loss on the initial margin deposit of €3,720 but has made a profit on the futures price of the shares of $9,920 (€10,416). In addition, the remaining euros he did not use, as a result of buying futures instead of fully paid cash equities, means he also has a positive interest return on his remaining funds as well as no currency exposure on this signifi-cant amount of money.

Note also that the fund manager could of course have simply left his initial margin in euros and deposited that with the clearing house. In this case, he would have to deposit slightly more money to cover the overall risk of currency depreciation, but equally his risk would be limited to effectively being capital-ized in the cost of his investment rather than impacting on his cash capital holding.

SWITCHING STOCK EXPOSURE

SSFs permit investors to move their existing cash exposure in one equity into exposure on an entirely different equity within the same (or indeed a different) sector. Using SSFs this transaction can be achieved more cash-efficiently and more cheaply than if investors wished to sell their core equity holding. Indeed, investors may be keen to keep their long-term equity holding, but be looking for a short-term readjustment relative to a similar equity in the sector, for instance. This approach also avoids any potential taxation issue in respect of capital gains on the core cash equity holding.

COVERED WRITES

Covered call-writing

Options traders and cash equity holders looking to increase the return from their shareholdings have for many years practised the strategy of selling covered calls. This strategy involves the purchase of a share and the sale of a call option—usually at an out-of-the-money strike price. The premium income gained from the call option improves the return on the shares.

Using SSFs, this strategy can be rendered even more cash-efficient because margin is paid to buy the futures as opposed to the full capital expenditure required to hold the cash. The premium gained from the option remains the same, thus making the return potentially higher in percentage terms than the extent of capital risked (i.e., the rate of return is larger due to the lower amount of the initial investment). However, if the share price falls, the resulting fall in the value of the SSF will also be a greater percentage decline, because the position is geared through margin—although the actual physical extent of the losses will be the same as those suffered by the holder of the underlying shares. Of course, investors who want to alleviate the gearing issue can deposit cash equivalent to the value of purchasing the underlying stock, in which case their returns will be enhanced by the interest return on the cash deposited. Note also that a short options position that is exercised will result in the seller having to deliver the underlying stock, while many SSFs are cash settled at expiry. Therefore, traders may find it preferable to trade out of their positions before they reach settlement in this instance.

On occasions—when financial markets have been especially busy or when a quiet period is looming—selling options is particularly attractive because time decay provides income by the day, as long as the option does not go into the money and gain intrinsic value. However, the problem with simply selling options is that there are potentially unlimited risks if the position goes wrong, and often retail investors are discouraged from entering positions that they might not be able to monitor as regularly as a professional trader.

Time decay affects all options. As options move closer to expiry, their likelihood of having greater value (i.e., their strike price being "in the money" or achieving greater profitability) declines, thus causing the value of the option to decline as well. The process of covered call-writing is intended to allow a trader to hold a long position and garner income from the short option position as it becomes less valuable.

Therefore, when investors see an options premium that they believe will expire worthless, the simplest route to profiting from the sold premium is to use an SSF to create a "covered call write". This process involves buying a future and selling a call of the same stock against the futures position.

Given that the equity market endured a period of remarkable volatility during 2001 and 2002, the usual prerequisite calmness (or relative calm) has been largely absent for the preferred trading of covered calls at the time of writing. However, this also permits us to examine a situation that exemplifies just how covered call-writing can work, even in an adverse market—in this case before, during, and after the 09/11 tragedy, which provoked colossal volatility in the stock market.

Glaxo SmithKline stock futures on LIFFE could be bought at 2035 pence on July 2nd of this year (2000), and, in anticipation of a fairly quiet summer trading period, we could sell the 2000 pence (October) call for an additional 141 pence. This option was exercisable into stock at expiry in mid-October, presuming the share price remained about 2000. Provided the shares remained below 2141 on expiry, we would be in profit for this trade.

By the end of summer, the stock itself had declined to 1895, but the options were worth a mere 19 pence. Hardly an ideal result, but if the position had been closed out we would have lost 140 pence on our stock and gained 121 pence on our options, so we would have been marginally out of pocket. However, the major losses in time value are during the last month of an equity's life. Therefore, let's presume we held on to our position, hoping for a recovery in the underlying equity—but not such a significant recovery that it wiped out our potential profit!

Nobody could foresee the dreadful events of September 11th, and this position suffered accordingly. The options slumped to 2 pence; but, it is fairly unrealistic to think that we would have closed out the position in such a volatile market and held onto the SSF. Almost immediately, the market bounced back from this spike, and indeed GSK stock staged a recovery during October back to 1940 pence. Of course, the ravages of time ate away at the premium and it was worth barely 13 pence by October 15th.

Presuming drug stocks remained reasonably popular in the wake of germ warfare concerns, the likelihood was that we could hold our stock futures closer to expiry and look for a way to get out with the least possible loss prior to expiry. As things stand, the stock future was losing 95 pence, while the option made us 122 pence. Given the enormous volatility that had exploded in the interim, making this market not ideally suited to covered call-writing, the ease of use of SSFs would nonetheless still garner a profit.

At expiry, GSK traded at 1908, leaving us with a profit on our option of the entire premium, namely 141 pence. Alas, of course, our long futures position was also somewhat affected by the fall to 1908, and from our purchase level at 2035 we notched up a loss of 127 ticks. Hardly a total victory, but overall our position still netted some 14 ticks of clear profit, which is quite remarkable given the incredible volatility of markets in the wake of the 09/11 tragedy.

Overall, the best time for covered call options-trading is during relatively quiet sideways markets, when hopefully our long futures position will not move particularly, but the option decays neatly as time to expiry nears.

MANAGING CAPITAL EXPOSURES

By exploiting the margin advantages of SSFs, investors can hold a significant quantity of their assets in higher grade money market instruments, such while still garnering the benefits of equity investment returns. In this respect, fund managers can also manage their capital exposures very neatly through SSFs even if they have not already received all the funds they expected to have or wish to modify their portfolio without actually changing all their investments.

For instance, a fund manager with a portfolio of bonds wishes to orient himself more toward the equity market, but does not want to sell out of his cash bond holdings before they mature in three months' time. By using a modest amount of his cash float, he can actually purchase the requisite SSFs equivalent to his desired equity exposure, while maintaining his substantial holding of cash bonds. If he wants to reduce some of his bond exposure, he could also sell Government Bond futures against his cash bond holdings.

CASH FLOW MANAGEMENT

Similarly, investment fund managers (and indeed retail investors) may find themselves at a point where they wish to make an investment, but know that they may not have the full quantity of capital to achieve it until a later time period (the following month, for example). By buying an SSF, the investor can have the exposure he requires before the full amount of his capital reaches him, thus enabling an investment fund manager to efficiently maintain a fully invested portfolio at all times, as well as allowing him to interpolate his purchases ahead of time if he so desires. By using SSFs that can be neatly bought and sold in a liquid market environment all day long and settled immediately, the fund manager can always access cash very readily if he needs to pay money back for redemptions, etc.

CONVERSIONS AND REVERSALS

A commonplace fodder of equity options market-makers, these traditionally involve basically creating a synthetic long/short position and then hedging it against a cash equity position. With the development of SSFs, it is increasingly possible to employ SSFs instead of the cash equity leg. A conversion involves three legs:

- sell a call;
- buy a put at the same strike (i.e., creating a synthetic short position);
- buy the SSF.

A reversal involves three slightly different legs to achieve the opposite result:

- buy a call;
- sell a put at the same strike (creating a synthetic long position);
- sell a future.

Essentially, the end result is a volatility-neutral and directionally-neutral trade. What you are doing here is trying to lock in a profit on entry, by exploiting the profit difference between the synthetic options position and the futures position. Presuming the pricing differential can be exploited on entry into the position, then you will be left with a profit on expiry. However, remember that the extent of the mis-pricing, which dictates your profit, will need to be sufficient to cover the brokerage cost of three separately executed legs of a position. Also, if you don't want to end up going to delivery on a physically settled exchange, then you will also need to be able to trade out of the position ahead of expiry and pay the concomitant profits while still netting a profit! Conversions and reversals are standard fodder for market-makers who have almost negligible costs of execution. Other traders may simply find they cannot access the market cheaply enough to make any money from these trades.

COVERED COMBINATIONS

There are multiplicitous variations that can be employed in the business of multi-legged SSFs strategies. For the purposes of this chapter we will use one example—the covered combination—which has various elements to it, but gives a flavour of just how almost any potential pay-off can be created using various options legs and indeed SSFs.

Naturally, the naked writing of options is a dangerous game, especially if the markets turn volatile. Similarly, covered writing (as we saw above) can leave you exposed if the market turns against your core futures position. How can you cover yourself further? Well, one thing you can employ is a covered combination. Essentially, you buy the SSF and sell a (covered) call against it. Then, to try and receive some more premium and garner some downside protection, you can sell a short put. Generally the call is at or just out of the money (i.e., below the current stock price) for the write. The put is typically just out of the money.

The put is typically selected at a strike below the current stock price ... but, here is the rub: essentially you ought to be fairly happy to buy the stock at this strike price if the position does not work as intended. Some investors may find this an impossible risk and therefore not wish to be involved in such a trade. However, the position overall is not too dangerous, although it is much more a strategy for consenting adults as opposed to elementary traders.

Let's say we want to buy General Motors at $36.00. So we could buy 1 contract of General Motors futures at $36.00, then:

Sell 1 April 40 calls at $1.60

Sell 1 April 30 puts at $1.40

If the future is at 36, the we have some 160 ticks of protection to the downside—in other words about 5% of the stock's value could be lost. Alas, not all markets are quite so volatile as the US stock market was during 2002, on which this hypothesis is based! By selling the puts, we gain a further 140 ticks of protection, meaning we have essentially a long futures position at an effective 310 ticks below the purchase price! In other words, a price of $33.

Of course, if the stock goes below $30, then you would expect to be assigned on your puts and you end up a further 100 shares long at $30 dollars, in addition to your 100 shares equivalent in the SSF at a net $33. So, you are averaging into a position on 200 shares at $31.50. Of course if the stock falls further, then suddenly the gloss on this trade evaporates rapidly, as you start losing on the equivalent of 200 shares or $200 per point. On the other hand, on the upside your gains will ultimately be capped by the short put, so you can make no more than $3,629.

AND FINALLY A QUICK TRADING TIP ...

We'll be brief in this section. For one thing there are a multiplicity of books out there that can already tell you how to profit from employing a vast multitude of technical analysis methods. Very, very simply, they all work with SSFs, so we see no need to reintroduce them here in our ham-fisted fashion when others have already written about them much more eloquently!

However, we do want to bring your attention to one quick and dirty indicator that can be of great benefit for traders in the short term, which we feel has a useful impact on the trading of SSFs.

The put/call ratio is a brilliant little indicator of where the interest is in a market and, generally speaking, when one type of options (calls or puts) has a lot more interest showing; this tends to point to a market imbalance. As a rough rule of thumb, usually if there is twice as much open interest (i.e., open positions) in calls as puts, then this is a good indicator that the bullish camp has got overwrought and a short-term pullback is possible. In other words, look to sell the SSF for one or perhaps two days, as the market rebalances itself. Likewise, when the puts are showing twice as much open interest compared with the calls, then buying the SSF is a good idea, as you will likely see a one- or perhaps a two-day bounce. Incidentally, if the market moves sharply in your favour over one day, then we tend to prefer taking our money and running.

CONCLUSION

This chapter has outlined many uses of SSFs. As ought to be clearly evident, the total number of possible uses basically depends on the level of human ingenuity seen in the SSFs marketplace. Overall, there is a vast range of different uses and approaches for deploying SSFs in retail and institutional investment portfolios, as well as a wide-ranging array of uses for traders. It is not unreasonable to state that SSFs truly add a whole new dimension to equity-trading.

4
Corporate Actions

Perhaps one of the most significant issues with Single Stock Futures (SSFs) is that their underlying fundamentals can change as a result of various corporate actions, either instituted by the company itself or as a result of third-party action. Companies can take over other companies or themselves be taken over. When they are taken over their listings tend to lapse, but there many possibilities for the number of shares outstanding if the acquiring company does not simply pay cash for the company it seeks to acquire. Moreover, mergers can entirely change the nature of a company's share structure. Meanwhile, even outside the realm of mergers and takeovers, companies have many ways of changing their fundamental share structure. They may choose to amalgamate shares (scrip issues) or issue more shares to raise cash by means of a rights issue. All of these issues affect the fundamentals of SSFs, and therefore it is worth looking at a series of examples in terms of the workings of many corporate actions. Preparedness is everything in trading, and, in this respect, understanding corporate actions in advance can be very beneficial, as that way you won't be surprised by events when they take place. The important thing to ensure is that when the underlying basis changes, then it will be mirrored in the SSF contract. Wherever possible, we have included a real-world example from the world of SSFs.

When stocks change a fundamental aspect of their make-up, as a result of corporate actions, the impact on SSFs (and indeed other related derivatives such as options) tend to be short lived. For already listed contracts (NQLX, OneChicago, and LIFFE, for instance) two quarterly months and two serial months tend to be affected, while new contracts will be listed according to the new contract specification. Note also that exchanges may sometimes opt to change back month futures where there is no open interest. Of course a very key issue here is not to get caught spreading two contracts that may have different fundamentals. For instance, if (as we will see) one month of an SSF has an underlying equivalent of 1,114 shares instead of the more common 1,000 due to a ratio adjustment, then of course we need to pay close attention to making any calendar spread relationship directly proportional in terms of the number of underlying shares rather than the number of contracts.

The key date for corporate actions is the "ex" date. In the case of dividends, for instance, if a share goes "ex-dividend" on March 1st, all purchasers of the stock before that date are entitled to the dividend and anybody buying after that date is not eligible for the dividend, even though it may be some weeks before the dividend is actually received by shareholders. With some announcements—such as pre-agreed mergers or friendly takeovers—the effect may be almost instantaneous, effective from the next trading day. Of course, in the event of such sudden announcements, a suspension in an underlying share ahead of such an announcement will also result in a simultaneous freezing in trading of derivatives, whether SSFs or options.

This chapter aims to discuss how this key issue, regarding the propensity of being able to change their spots in one form or another, differentiates individual equity derivatives from their commodity and financial cousins.

THE RATIO METHOD OF ADJUSTMENT—AN INTRODUCTION

Probably the most important thing to understand for corporate actions is the ratio method, probably the most commonly applied method of changing a contract's specification as a result of corporate action.

One of the most popular methods used in SSF (and indeed other exchange-traded equity derivatives) contracts is the "ratio approach". Note that this approach to remedying the external effects of a corporate action is not to be confused with "ratio spreads", which are beloved of options brokers the world over, because you pay some brokerage on multiple legs of a fairly complex strategy.

The main points to consider with the ratio adjustment concept include:

(1)   The physical price of the future will be amended.
(2)   The size of the contract (i.e., the number of underlying shares it represents) will change—therefore having an impact on spread-trading, because a ratio will be required to trade against the other share futures.
(3)   Ultimately, the contract size anomaly will be amended and will usually revert to the original size (e.g., 100 shares for international contracts on LIFFE or 1,000 shares for UK USF companies, and 100 shares on a US stock on a US exchange—the exception being India where contract sizes vary widely) when new contract months are listed. Occasionally, exchanges will amend the existing contracts earlier. This is most likely to occur if there is no open interest in a particular back month. Note, however, if there is no open interest in, say, a December back month

contract and the following March contract has open interest, then the exchange is unlikely to amend the earlier contract and keep the later contract at the amended size. However, in certain instances, very small quantities of open interest may be amended by negotiation, although this can of course be tricky to achieve for an exchange.

The most common uses of the ratio method are to make adjustments to contracts to account for corporate events such as stock splits or bonus/scrip issues.

Example 1: EXXON Mobil

During the middle of July 2001, when EXXON Mobil announced a subdivision of their share capital, the "ratio" method was applied to create a solution for existing contracts. Specifically, the ratio was 2 : 1 and the end result was as follows (as confirmed by LIFFE on July 18th): futures settlements would stand as they were on July 18th and then would change for July 19th.

Therefore, the contract size for existing EXXON Mobil SSFs grew from 100 shares to 200. This is, of course, the same process as would befall options in similar circumstances. However, traders should always remember that when new contracts are listed (i.e., any new months listed after July 19th when the change took place), the exchange will revert to the standard contract size of 100 shares per contract. Incidentally, the Dutch bank ING did precisely the same 2.0 ratio change at the end of June 2001.

Example 2: ENEL SpA

Earlier, in July 2001 (July 6th, effective July 9th), Italian oil/energy company ENEL did a similar thing while converting their share capital and redenominating the company into euros. Again, the ratio model was employed (Table 4.1) and this time it was at a level of 0.5 (i.e., the share price effectively doubled, while the contract itself halved to 50 shares from 100).

Table 4.1

Delivery month	Futures settlement price Friday 6 July 2001	Futures reference price Monday 9 July 2001
July 2001	€ 3.61	€ 7.22
August 2001	€ 3.62	€ 7.24
September 2001	€ 3.65	€ 7.30
December 2001	€ 3.69	€ 7.38

Overall, it isn't too difficult to understand the ratio method, but the important point is to look for the date the notice is implemented and therefore which new contract months will be subject to reversion to the standard size.

Margin changes in such moves are fairly simple to comprehend too, as they are also relative to the ratio adjustment. Essentially, the variation margin charged at the close of business on the first day of the modified contract's trading (e.g., Monday, May 21st for BT USFs) reflects the change from the adjusted reference price or (presuming the market traded that day) the traded price.

DEALING WITH DEMERGER

On 19th November 2001 there was a fairly spectacular upheaval in the European telecoms sector when the UK's long privatized carrier, British Telecom (nowadays more familiar by its initials BT), opted to split its companies in two as one way to try and break down what had long been perceived as a fairly plodding management approach, dating back to its days as a nationalized utility. One company, BT Group plc (ticker: BTL) would look after existing fixed-line services, while mmO_2 (ticker: MOO) would look after all the mobile telephony side of the business. To put in context just how huge this demerger was, both companies automatically qualified for London's benchmark FTSE 100 index—which tracks London's 100 largest shares and has a market capitalization of around £940,000 million at the time of writing in late 2002.

The existing BT share options were split into an underlying package of 1,000 shares for each component company (the underlying split was that one share became one share in each component). This applied to pre-existing strikes ahead of the demerger on November 19th, 2001. Given the popularity of BT shares (which were very much the people's shares thanks to the Thatcher government's privatization programme), the options remained trading in this fashion for all the existing strikes that were listed out to the expiry of the April 2002 series—in other words, some five months after the demerger deal went through. Likewise, Universal Stock Futures (USFs) were traded as a package until final expiry in December 2001.

Meanwhile, the Exchange Delivery Settlement Price (EDSP) for the existing USFs in pre-demerged BT was determined (December being the only month that remained) using official closing prices on the London Stock Exchange for both mmO_2 plc shares and BTG, using the following formula:

$$EDSP = mmO_2 \text{ plc share price} + BTG \text{ share price}$$

Although this book is primarily concerned with the world of SSFs, we cannot help but diverge for a moment into the options settlement arrangements for BT, as it reflects a veritable cornucopia of issues relating to just how much work can be required to provide a working derivatives market—and moreover how SSFs, being futures, can be much simpler to modify than single stock options. Given that the worlds of SSFs and equity options are so interlinked, it is worth looking at how options can provide a great many more issues than USFs, which retain their "simple and efficient" byline!

For one thing, BT options in November retained a slight carbuncle with a contract size of 1,114 lots and a wondrous array of strike prices between 296 pence and 718 pence, thanks to a previous rights issue (usually, they would run 280, 300, 330, 360, 390, etc. until 500 pence where the strikes would be 50 pence apart).

Fortunately, it was an even number for the demerger of the stock with a 1 : 1 ratio, so at least LIFFE could still create a settlement position of 1,000 shares for each underlying component.

Meanwhile, the other options settlement months (until April, some five months away, lest we forget) were settled according to Table 4.2 for each stock value.

Interestingly, on commencement of "when issued"-trading (November 9th, 2001), the new mmO_2 options traded an impressive 3,000 contracts. The new USF contracts were issued from November 14th.

Of course, the interesting issue here was that in the event of "when issued"-trading not resulting in admission to the "official list", then LIFFE would have been forced to declare all derivative trades null and void—consistent with the LSE rules on the issue (LIFFE offered "when issued"-dealing for equity options only, not USFs). Therefore, the options and USFs were declared "conditional" contracts until the new companies had acceded to the "official list" of the LSE. Sometimes one has to both admire and indeed feel sorry for the hoops through which derivatives product dervishes must jump in order to maintain an orderly market! Indeed, this guide only scratches the issues in many respects. *On the other hand, one thing that is beneficial about cash-settled SSFs is that dealers don't end up having to enter the relative purdah[1] of odd lot-dealing in order to achieve successful delivery as can be the case with some of the more complex mathematical resolutions of SSF rationalizations!*

On the trading front, the great advantage with LIFFE USF products was of course the fact that, as soon as the announcement was made, traders could find an easy way to short the company, lest they felt that the initial reaction to the demerger had been merely a "relief rally" that the much criticized BT management had finally made some sort of decision, even if it may not have been

---

[1] The practice of hiding behind a veil or a screen.

Table 4.2

Contract size	British Telecommunications plc exercise price	mmO₂ plc (pence per share)	BT Group plc (pence per share)
1,000	180	39	141
	200	44	156
	220	48	172
	240	52	188
	260	57	203
	280	61	219
	300	65	235
	330	72	258
	360	79	281
	390	85	305
	420	92	328
	460	100	360
	500	109	391
	550	120	430
	600	131	469
	650	142	508
	700	153	547
1,114	296	65	231
	323	70	253
	350	76	274
	377	82	295
	413	90	323
	449	98	351
	494	108	386
	539	118	421
	584	127	457
	629	137	492
	673	147	526
	718	157	561

ultimately the right one. Of such things are markets made, and indeed almost as soon as the demerger announcement was made, BT shares rallied somewhat from their 324 pence lows in the immediate aftermath of 09/11 and reached a rather juicy 385 pence on September 18th. A cunning sale at this moment would have resulted in a very handy profit on the day the conditional USFs were launched.

On November 12th, the BT price dropped to 310 pence, but, despite a rapid rally as investor interest seemed sound in the "when issued" market for mmO$_2$ equity options, even when the new separate USFs became available (for December 1st, January 2nd, February 2nd, March 2nd delivery), the position could still have been closed out at around 341 for a very healthy profit. So, if nothing else, it pays to understand such corporate actions, as there is definitely money to be made (and indeed lost if you are not careful) in the aftermath of the announcements—which usually create some volatility and, therefore, both opportunities and indeed dangers.

SHARE CAPITAL SUBDIVISION

Often more commonly known as a stock split: "an increase in the number of issued shares by dividing each existing share into two or more shares with a proportionately smaller nominal value.

Barclays adjustments

From Monday, April 29th, 2002, Barclays equity options and USF contracts on LIFFE were amended to cater for the subdivision of share capital. For every £1 nominal value share the holder received four shares, each with a nominal value of 25p. A 4:1 ratio was employed.

With SSFs the end result was simple—previously, contracts were for 1,000 shares, now they are for 4,000. Tables 4.3 and 4.4 demonstrate the differences in the changes, one for USFs and the other for individual Barclays options. With effect from Monday, April 29th, 2002, the lot size of existing Barclays

Table 4.3

Delivery month	Futures settlement price Friday 26 April 2002	Futures reference price Monday 29 April 2002
May 2002	2405.00	601.50
June 2002	2416.00	604.00
September 2002	2417.00	604.50

Table 4.4

Barclays plc exercise prices Friday 26 April 2002	Barclays plc exercise prices Monday 29 April 2002
1300	325
1350	338
1400	350
1450	363
1500	375
1600	400
1700	425
1800	450
1900	475
2000	500
2100	525
2200	550
2300	575
2400	600
2500	625
2600	650
2700	675
2800	700
2900	725
3000	750
3100	775
3200	800

equity option contracts became 4,000 shares. Exercise prices were adjusted as shown in Table 4.4. Options also became deliverable in 4,000 lot packages, as opposed to the normal 1,000 lots. However, all new contracts listed after April 29th, 2002 are in the more common 1,000 lot packages, and in the case of options at standard exercise prices.

Telefónica

Telefónica has had one of the more interesting stock splits with the company managing to have several bonus share issues during the life of some SSFs contracts. At its AGM on April 7th, 2000, the company passed a resolution to increase share capital through the completely free issue of one new share with full dividend rights for every fifty old shares. The first issue took place early in the year (2001), before SSFs were launched. As the pre-existing options contracts were amended to become 102 share contracts, the Telefónica SSFs were launched as 102 share contracts, Then, when the second issue took place a few months later, the 102 contracts became 104 share contracts!

Then, following a vote at the Annual General Shareholders Meeting held on June 15th, 2001, Telefónica SA did the same thing again in 2002. The first bonus issue was from January 25th to February 8th and the second one was from March 22nd to April 5, 2002 (both inclusive).

Once again, as in 2001, the bonus issue involved shareholders being given one new share with full dividend rights for every fifty old shares. The allocation took place between March 22nd and April 5th, 2002 (all dates are inclusive), and this led to a further amendment to the SSFs and equity options contracts at MEFF, where Telefónica has been one of the world's most actively traded SSFs.

Rather than examine every change, as the principle is the same, let's look at this modification. The amendment to the SSFs contracts was as follows: each open position in an existing Telefónica contract (as of March 22nd, 2002, this was June, September, and December, 2002) became a position in 104 shares (i.e., $51/50 \times 102$ shares $= 104$). There being no open interest in the March 2003 contract on the day before the adjustment, it remained a contract for 100 shares. In other words, the ratio method was deployed here on the basis of:

$$\text{Number of shares represented by one contract} \times \frac{\text{Shares after}}{\text{Shares before}}$$

In order to retain the notional value of the positions before and after this adjustment, a specific pair of prices, namely the closing price of the position and subsequent registered price, had to be used. The closing price of the 102 share contracts and the registered price of the 104 share contracts worked on the following equation:

102 shares×Closing price of the position (after marking to market

the session of March 21st)

$= 104$ shares $\times$ Registered price (new opening price)

This solution is notable, because there are multiple solutions for the closing price and the registered price, and the pair to be chosen was the one closest to the settlement price of March 21st.

Just to ensure that everybody is clear about this process (which is aimed at providing a fair price that amounts to the same value for both packages of shares), let's look at that issue again, with a hypothetical example. For instance, if the settlement price on March 21st had been 13.40, the pair of prices used to close and subsequently open the futures positions would be 13.52 and 13.26 (13.52 × 102 = 13.26 ∗ 104—i.e. a capital value of 1379.04 for the whole contract).

Therefore, MEFF would settle the positions at 13.40 on March 21st. On the next day, before the session starts, the 102 share contracts would be closed at 13.52 and the positions instead transferred into new 104 share contracts, which would be opened at a price of 13.26 (although naturally this doesn't mean they have to trade there).

So, if a MEFF trader had a position long in the SSF at 13.40, he ought to be long after the adjustment at a price of 13.40 × 50/51 = 13.137 254 901 9 with a 104.04 multiplier. However, as the position has been closed at 13.52, this "benefit" compensates for the fact that, instead of being long at 13.137 254 901 9, the trader will instead be long at 13.26 (and of course that his contract multiplier is 104.04 and not 104).

On 4 March 2003, another contract adjustment was made to Telefónica for a further share capital increase. The ratio approach was once again used and the futures settlement price for Tuesday March 11th was determined by multiplying the futures settlement price on Monday 10th March by the inverse of the adjustment ratio. Thus, the reference prices were as follows:

Delivery month	Futures settlement price Monday 10 March 2003	Futures reference price Tuesday 11 March 2003
March 2003	8.11	7.95
April 2003	8.13	7.97
May 2003	8.14	7.98
June 2003	8.17	8.01

Once again Telefónica ended up with odd-sized contracts. In this case, with effect from Tuesday 11 March 2003, the contract size of the March 2003, April 2003 and June 2003 delivery months in respect of Telefónica SA Universal Stock Futures Contracts became 104 shares per lot and the contract size of the May 2003 delivery month for Telefónica SA Universal Stock Futures Contracts became 102 shares per lot. All delivery months listed on or after Tuesday 11 March 2003 reverted to a standard contract size of 100 shares per lot.

CHANGING NAME

CGNU changes name

Thankfully, the brand consultants haven't got to governments or commodity markets yet, so we have been spared the burden of having to consider renaming

US Treasury Bonds, wheat, and so forth. Although naturally this may yet happen! On the other hand, some of the world's corporations often indulge in a change of name, which, if nothing else, means that almost overnight one can become confused about just what one is trading. The UK insurer CGNU recently fell foul of the rebranding army by changing its name from CGNU plc to Aviva—which apparently is meant to make the company sound more lively ... Anyway, the name change came into effect in July 2002, so the underlying contracts retained the CGNU name until then. There was no impact on the pricing of SSFs, although this was one instance where, regardless of open interest, the contract was changed immediately in accordance with the corporate action!

SPECIAL DIVIDENDS

Telia special dividend

Occasionally companies decide to return some capital to their shareholders in the shape of a special dividend. This may be as a result of a multitude of circumstances, such as a desire to reduce capital thanks to a change in corporate strategy or as a way of rewarding shareholders after the spin-off of a subsidiary.

Of somewhat more substantive fiscal interest, the Scandinavian telecoms company, Telia, paid a special dividend at the end of April 2002. While SSF contracts do not reflect dividends in any form, the special dividend issue is one that is reflected in the price of the contract *per se* (as opposed to the normal dividend which goes through a period of priced-in discounting without contract modification). So, with Telia paying out SEK 0.10, the "reduction method" was applied. I have always rather liked the "reduction method", as it merely involves picking a date and then reducing the contract value by the amount of the dividend. In this case, the futures reference price on Wednesday, April 24th was calculated by taking the settlement price on Tuesday, April 23rd and taking 10 Swedish öre away from it. The net result is shown in Table 4.5 for all months. Of course, the futures reference price affected all variation margin charges for that day.

Table 4.5

Delivery month	Futures settlement price Tuesday 23 April 2003	Futures reference price Wednesday 24 April 2003
May 2002	SEK 32.91	SEK 32.81
June 2002	SEK 32.75	SEK 32.65
July 2002	SEK 32.87	SEK 32.77
September 2002	SEK 33.13	SEK 33.03

Early dividend payment

Telecom Italia Mobile SpA (TIM), the Italian cellphone giant, somewhat surprised the market on November 7th, 2002 with an announcement of its plans to pay an early dividend of €0.1865 per share on December 19th, 2002. with the expectation of ex-dividend trading from December 16th, 2002. The company described the dividend as being part of the full year dividend to be made in 2003, although some reports termed this payment a "special dividend".

However, Euronext LIFFE decided, after consultations with TIM, that as the company had described the dividend as being part of the full year dividend (and not a "special dividend"), therefore no adjustment needed to be made to *TIM USFs contracts to cater for this event.*

Some might think this a little harsh, but a quick look at the Euronext LIFFE exchange's Corporate Events Policy, issued on February 1st, 2001, provided key criteria (essentially similar across all exchanges, but traders always need to pay close attention to specifics relating to the markets they trade!) that Euronext LIFFE use in deciding whether a dividend shall be considered a special dividend:

(a)   the declaration by a company of a dividend additional to those dividends declared as part of the company's normal results and dividend reporting cycle (merely an adjustment to the timing of the declaration of a company's expected dividend would not be considered as a special dividend circumstance); or

(b)   the identification of an element of a cash dividend, paid in line with a company's normal results and dividend reporting cycle, that is unambiguously additional to the company's normal payment.

Telecom Italia dividend

On November 8th, 2002, the day after the TIM announcement, the fixed-line Italian telecom company Telecom Italia SpA announced plans for an early dividend payment of €0.1357 per share to be paid on December 19th, 2002 and an expected ex-dividend date of December 16th. Once again, while some reports termed this a "special dividend" the company regarded the dividend as being part of the full year dividend to be made in 2003. Once again LIFFE consulted Telecom Italia for confirmation and like the TIM dividend, Euronext LIFFE decided that *no adjustments would be made to Telecom Italia SpA USFs contracts to cater for this event.* The same criteria as mentioned above in relation to TIM were employed to make this decision.

SMALLER TICK SIZES

Ever attentive to customer demand, LIFFE made some fine-tuning changes to its existing Vodafone options and USFs early in 2002. From Thursday, April 18th, options expiry was extended to two years and two serial expiry months were introduced to allow for the first three calendar months always being available for trading in one of Europe's most heavily traded companies. Of perhaps more significance to traders of USFs, at the same time, LIFFE announced that from May 20th, the minimum price increment in the mobile telephone company would be reduced from 0.5 pence to 0.25 pence for all USF and individual options transactions. This is of course very interesting, as again this was an announcement the exchange could make unilaterally without having to wait for existing contracts to expire. Traders with positions in any form of equity derivatives therefore need to make sure they keep abreast of such developments and watch for corporate announcements from the companies whose SSFs they have positions in. The exchanges usually post their corporate actions announcements on their websites as soon as they are available, and traders are advised to ensure that they keep a keen eye out for such changes. Note of course that while exchanges can make certain moves unilaterally, they are invariably done after consulting with leading market players to ascertain their feelings on such changes. Indeed, moves such as the reduction in Vodafone's tick size and the addition of delivery months to the cycle were expressly as a result of demand coming from market participants.

Subsequently, on November 5th, 2002, Euronext LIFFE further amended their tick sizes on various British SSFs. Note that while the exchange didn't put this into effect untiul November 11th, 2002, it was still a fairly short notice period. Traders need to keep paying close attention to all exchange announcements of this sort, lest they are caught out by these announcements. In this case, the minimum price movement of some six UK stocks was changed from 0.5 pence to 0.25 pence (Table 4.6).

Several other minimum price movements were adjusted by LIFFE in early 2003. With effect from Monday 10th March, the USFs of Barclays and Shell Transport & Trading were reduced to a 0.25-pence tick size from 0.5.

EDSP CHANGES

Also in the category of amendments the exchange can impose, although they are not as a result of corporate actions by the SSF-listed companies themselves, are trading hours and the settlement process. Whether cash-settled or deliverable, exchanges will infrequently make fine-tuning adjustments to their contracts in order to try and maximize interest and maintain as fair a pricing

Table 4.6   Universal Stock Futures.

Contract	Trade Registered System code	Current tick size	New tick size
BT Group plc	BTL	0.5	0.25
Legal & General Group plc	LGN	0.5	0.25
Marks & Spencer Group plc	MKS	0.5	0.25
mmO$_2$ plc	MMO*	0.5	0.25
Sainsbury (J) plc	SBR	0.5	0.25
Tesco plc	TSC	0.5	0.25

*The TRS or Trade Registration System code for a stock on a futures exchange like Euronext LIFFE may be different from its "ticker symbol" (i.e., what one deals in on the London Stock Exchange). Here, MOO is this ticker symbol, but MMO is the TRS symbol for the Universal Stock Future.

model as possible. For instance, when LIFFE issued Irish stocks, it soon realized that the initial EDSP chosen was not really the best market indicator. The initial EDSP was the official closing price of the Irish Stock Exchange in Dublin. In its stead, LIFFE opted to replace this EDSP method with the closing auction on the Irish Stock Exchange between 16:28 and 16:30 (London time) to determine the daily settlement price. In the event that no auction takes place, our dear old friend VWAP (the Volume Weighted Average Price of all trades between 16:13 and 16:28 London time) is deployed.

EARLY INTRODUCTION OF CONTRACTS

In the increasingly competitive exchange landscape, there was an interesting development, prompted by a request from an exchange member who wished to transact business ahead of the contract's official listing. In this instance, during 2002, LIFFE brought forward the introduction of the Total Fina Elf USF for December 2002 to Friday, April 26th. Naturally, LIFFE is keen to gain market share and transact business, while the member evidently wanted to benefit from exchange-traded central counterparty clearing and so forth, as opposed to trading over the counter (of course, one or more prospective counterparties may even have been banned from trading outside the established regulated exchanges). This early introduction of a series was interesting for two reasons: most notably, this contract was not scheduled to be listed until Friday, June 28th, 2002 and bringing its listing forward meant that it was introduced several days before the June contract was listed on Tuesday, April 30th.

MERGER

During October 2002, the Scandinavian telco market was rationalized with the merger of Sonera Corporation and Telia AB. Euronext LIFFE issued a notice on October 22nd, detailing the exchange's intentions over the proposed merger. Note that proposed mergers leave exchanges in a precarious position, as in the event of the merger not being consummated, the exchange needs to be able to offer a fallback position to allow continuous trading in both companies' shares.

The merger was effected by means of an exchange, whereby shareholders in Sonera received 1.514 40 Telia shares (stock exchange code "TLS1V") in exchange for each Sonera share held. Subject to the completion of the merger, Telia announced plans to change its name to TeliaSonera:

- Telia shareholders would retain their shares in Telia Ordinary SEK 3.20 shares. Upon completion of the merger, Telia shares stock exchange symbol on the Stockholm Stock Exchange changed to TLSN.
- Sonera shareholders who accepted the exchange offer were issued with one Sonera-exchanged share for every Sonera share held. Sonera-exchanged shares then commenced trading on the pre-list of the Helsinki Stock Exchange on Friday, November 15th, 2002.
- Then, when the meger offer was successfully completed, Sonera-exchanged-share shareholders had their holding converted on the basis of 1.514 40 Telia shares for every Sonera-exchanged share held. Telia shares then commenced trading on the Helsinki Stock Exchange on Monday, December 2nd, 2002.

As you can see from the above series of movements, mergers can be protracted in their settlement, and thus the possibility for the merger not to happen leaves exchanges open to a potential problem if the merger comes undone. In this instance, the exchange offered the rather blunt explanation: "If the exchange offer is not completed, Sonera-exchanged shares will be converted back into Sonera shares as soon as practically possible." Given the various stages involved in this merger, perhaps it's not difficult to understand why!

Given the way the merger was being effected in the underlying cash market, this resulted in the Telia USFs continuing to be listed on Euronext LIFFE, while Sonera's USFs were suspended—a decision made somewhat easier by the fact that there was no open interest in the existing Sonera USF contracts on the date of the announcement.

Dealings in the newly merged company started on Monday, December 9th. The change to LIFFE's USFs was to redesignate the code for Telia shares as TLSN (to represent the newly merged company). The lot size remained the same and the settlement price was also unchanged ahead of the new dealings, although the Telia USFs were renamed TeliaSonera in line with the new title of the company. Sonera futures (the first event of its kind in which two international stock futures-listed companies merged) were suspended after the merger announcement and their futures were not reintroduced. With the commencement of trading on December 9th in the newly merged company, the USFs on Sonera were delisted.

RIGHTS ISSUES

The UK-based insurer Legal & General Group plc (LGEN) announced its intention to pursue a rights issue on September 18th, 2002. Shareholders received the right to purchase 13 new LGEN ordinary 2.5-pence shares, at a price of 60 pence per share, for every 50 LGEN ordinary 2.5-pence shares held. The company also noted that these new shares issued under the rights would not be eligible for the interim dividend, which was due to be paid on October 1st, 2002. The ratio approach was used to determine the adjustments. The adjustment ratio was calculated using the official closing share price of LGEN ordinary 2.5-pence shares on Thursday, September 26th, 2002, the rights issue price, and excluding the announced interim dividend of 1.67 pence per share, because this went ex-dividend on September 11th before the rights announcement was made. The adjustment ratio was to be calculated as follows:

$$\text{Ratio} = \frac{(50 \times \text{LGEN cum event share price}) + (13 \times 60 \text{ pence})}{63 \times \text{LGEN cum event share price}}$$

The LGEN closing share price on Thursday, September 26th, 2002 was 100.5 pence, and as a consequence the ratio used to determine contract adjustments was 0.9168. Therefore, with effect from Friday, September 27th, 2002, the lot size of existing LGEN USFs contract delivery months became 1,091 shares. Details of futures settlement prices for LGEN USFs contracts on Thursday, September 26th, 2002 and of the resulting futures reference prices in respect of variation margin calculations for Friday, September 27th, 2002 are shown in Table 4.7.

Table 4.7

Delivery month	Futures settlement price Thursday 26 September 2002	Futures reference price Friday 27 September 2002
October 2002	102.50	94.00
November 2002	102.50	94.00
December 2002	103.50	95.00
March 2003	104.50	96.00

Additional USFs contract delivery months introduced for trading on LGEN ordinary 2.5-pence shares on and after Friday, September 27th, 2002 had a standard contract size of 1,000 shares per lot. Once again, traders need to beware of this when spread-trading as naturally being short (long) on a 1,091 contract against a long (short) 1,000 lot contract leaves the trader open to some rather nasty potential consequences.

Zurich Financial Services AG

On October 14th, 2002, Zurich Financial Services AG (ZURN) proposed a rights issue. Shareholders would receive the right to purchase two new ZURN ordinary CHF 10 shares, at a price of CHF 65 per share, for every three ZURN ordinary CHF 10 shares held. ZURN shares commenced trading ex-rights on Thursday, October 17th, 2002. Our dear friend—the ratio approach—was employed, and the adjustment ratio was calculated using the official closing share price of ZURN ordinary CHF 10 shares on Wednesday, October 16th, 2002. The rights issue price was calculated as follows:

$$\text{Ratio} = \frac{(3 \times \text{ZURN cum event share price}) + (2 \times \text{CHF } 65)}{5 \times \text{ZURN cum event share price}}$$

The ZURN closing share price on Wednesday, October 16th, 2002 was CHF 157, and as a consequence the ratio used to determine contract adjustments was 0.7656. Therefore, with effect from Thursday, October 17th, 2002, the lot size of existing ZURN USFs contract delivery months became 131 shares. Details of futures settlement prices for ZURN USFs contracts on Wednesday, October 16th, 2002 and of the resulting futures reference prices in respect of variation margin calculations for Thursday, October 17th, 2002 are shown in Table 4.8.

As ever, additional USFs contract delivery months introduced for trading on ZURN ordinary CHF 10 shares on and after Thursday, October 17th, 2002 have a standard contract size of 100 shares per lot.

Table 4.8

Delivery month	Futures settlement price Wednesday 16 October 2002	Futures reference price Thursday 17 October 2002
October 2002	CHF 163.3	CHF 125.0
November 2002	CHF 163.3	CHF 125.0
December 2002	CHF 163.4	CHF 125.1
March 2003	CHF 163.7	CHF 125.3

Citigroup Inc.

Proposed distribution of Travelers Property Casualty Corporation shares to Citigroup Inc. shareholders

On August 19th, 2002, Citigroup Inc. (CIT) announced a distribution of Travelers Property Casualty Corporation (TPC) shares to CIT shareholders. Under the terms of the distribution initially announced, CIT shareholders received 0.043 042 2 class "A" shares of common stock $0.01 in TPC and 0.088 432 6 class "B" shares of common stock $0.01 in TPC for each share of common stock $0.01 held in CIT. The ex-distribution date was Wednesday, August 21st, 2002.

The adjustment ratio was calculated using the cum distribution share price of CIT shares, a value determined by the Exchange based on the price of CIT shares prior to the settlement time of CIT USFs contracts on Tuesday, August 20th, 2002 and the "when issued" share price of TPC class "A" and class "B" shares on Tuesday, August 20th, 2002 at this time.

The adjustment ratio for CIT USFs contracts was therefore calculated as follows based on a distribution ratio:

$$\text{Ratio} = \frac{C - (0.0430422 \times A) - (0.0884326 \times B)}{C}$$

where

$$A = \text{TPC class "A" share price}$$
$$B = \text{TPC class "B" share price}$$
$$C = \text{CIT cum event share price}$$

However, Citibank subsequently announced a slightly different rights distribution ratio on August 20th: a combination of 0.043 204 3 class "A" shares of common stock $0.01 in TPC and 0.088 765 6 class "B" shares of common stock $0.01 in TPC for each share of common stock $0.01 held in CIT. As a consequence of this revision the adjustment ratio for CIT USFs contracts was ultimately calculated as:

$$\text{Ratio} = \frac{C - (0.0432043 \times A) - (0.0887656 \times B)}{C}$$

The contract adjustments would be made by applying the ratio method on the basis of the cum distribution share price of CIT shares prior to the settlement time of CIT USFs contracts on Tuesday, August 20th, 2002 and the "when issued" share price of TPC class "A" and class "B" shares at this time.

The "when issued" share price of TPC class "A" shares and TPC class "B" shares, used to determine the adjustment ratio, were $16.95 and $18.66, respectively. CIT shares' cum distribution share price, used to determine the

Table 4.9

Delivery month	Futures settlement price Tuesday 20 August 2002	Futures reference price Wednesday 21 August 2002
September 2002	$35.67	$33.28
October 2002	$35.72	$33.32
November 2002	$35.71	$33.31
December 2002	$35.71	$33.31

adjustment ratio, was $35.60. As a consequence, the ratio used to determine contract adjustments was 0.9329.

Details of futures settlement prices for CIT USFs contracts on Tuesday, August 20th, 2002, and of the resulting futures reference prices in respect of variation margin calculations for Wednesday, August 21st, 2002 are shown in Table 4.9.

Once again, traders need to beware of such contract adjustments, as companies can change their minds, and such amendments to these contracts can be perilous to your financial health!

SHARE CAPITAL INCREASE

When France Telecom announced on Monday 24 March 2003 a share capital increase, it had an interesting twist. The core rights issue was aimed at raising some 16 billion dollars and took the form of a free issuance of warrants to existing shareholders. It marked the biggest rights issue ever seen in Europe. Each shareholder received one warrant for each share held at the close of trading on Monday 24 March 2003. The warrants were exercisable from Tuesday 25 March 2003 to Friday 4 April 2003 inclusive and permitted each shareholder to subscribe to 19 new France Telecom Ordinary €4 shares, at a subscription price of €14.50, for each 20 warrants held (the closing price of the underlying shares by comparison was €20 on 24 March). The warrants themselves were traded on the Premier Marché of Euronext Paris from Tuesday 25 March 2003 to Friday 4 April 2003 inclusive with France Telecom trading ex-event from Tuesday 25 March 2003.

Our old friend the ratio method was deployed for this amendment. The adjustment ratio was calculated using the official closing share price of France Telecom Ordinary €4 shares on Monday 24 March 2003 and the subscription price was as follows:

$$\text{Ratio} = \frac{(20 \times \text{France Telecom cum-event share price}) + (19 \times 14.50)}{39 \times \text{France Telecom cum-event share price}}$$

The France Telecom USFs reference price for variation margin calculated on Tuesday 25 March 2003 was determined by multiplying the France Telecom USFs settlement price of Monday 24 March 2003 by this ratio . The lot size of existing France Telecom USFs delivery months was adjusted by being multiplied by the inverse of this ratio. The France Telecom closing share price on Monday 24 March 2003 was €20 and in consequence the ratio used to determine contract adjustments was 0.86602. With effect from Tuesday 25 March 2003 the contract size of existing France Telecom USFs Contracts became 115 shares per lot.

Details of futures settlement prices for France Telecom USFs Contracts on Monday 24 March 2003 and of the resulting futures reference prices, in respect of variation margin calculations for Tuesday 25 March 2003, were as follows:

Delivery month	Futures settlement price Monday 24 March 2003	Futures reference price Tuesday 25 March 2003
March 2003	19.54	16.92
April 2003	19.59	16.97
May 2003	19.63	17.00
June 2003	19.46	16.85

Variation margin was also affected by this corporate event. France Telecom USFs Contracts daily settlement prices determined up to and including Monday 24 March 2003 reflected cum-event trading of France Telecom Ordinary €4 shares. Daily Settlement Prices determined on and from Tuesday 25 March 2003 reflected ex-event trading of France Telecom Ordinary €4 shares. Variation margin calculated at the close of business on Tuesday 25 March 2003 reflected the contract price movement from the adjusted USFs traded price (had no trading taken place the reference price would have been used instead). As ever all new France Telecom contracts issued on and after Tuesday 25 March 2003 reverted to the standard contract size of 100 shares per lot.

CONCLUSION

Stock-restructuring is a fact of life. By having an understanding of the basic concepts, life should be a lot less stressful for traders when other, similar changes occur! True, the bias of corporate announcements can vary according to the market cycle, but, nonetheless, all announcements tend to take place on a fairly regular basis. In bull markets, takeovers and mergers may be more popular than in bear phases, when restructuring and cost-cutting may be to the fore. Rights issues can be popular irrespective of the market situation, although they tend to be a bit more likely when values are high, allowing companies to issue stock at what they regard as a healthy price. With SSFs really only starting to take off since 2000, when the dotcom bubble was bursting, we have yet to complete a full cycle in the liquid SSFs markets. However, a glance around the world reveals examples of almost every key issue in the lexicon of corporate announcements even as early as this in the development of SSFs as a key global trading instrument.

5
Users of Single Stock Futures

Research has traditionally found that when futures trading has been introduced to a market, there is usually a reduction in volatility and transaction costs, which further enhances liquidity and allows people to more actively trade the market. This will allow for a multitude of strategies, some of which we may not yet envision.

Mark Rzepczynski (2002)

The intriguing thing about the creation of Single Stock Futures (SSFs) is that while the overall exchange-traded derivatives market is increasingly a mature one, SSFs provide a vast series of opportunities for existing market users. Indeed, as liquidity grows and more innovative players enter the market, it is going to be intriguing to see just how the whole product range expands. In this chapter, we are going to look at a series of different market participants and see how they can approach the SSF marketplace to find new ways of making their life easier or more profitable ...

THE NEED FOR LIQUIDITY

However, before we get carried away, the first thing we really need is liquidity. At the time of writing, the US SSFs market has barely been born. The most successful SSFs markets to date have been the MEFF in Spain, India's NSE, and at Euronext LIFFE. Nevertheless, none have yet been truly stunning successes (although MEFF has been the greatest achiever in recent times). Without a solid core basis of liquidity, SSFs futures run the risk of being stillborn. The US, European, and Indian markets have all had relatively different approaches to boosting liquidity.

One key issue in the development of all equity futures markets has been the requirement to have market participants who have access to both cash and futures markets. In the case of the Sydney Futures Exchange, for instance, it had a pool of liquidity providers based in the fixed income and money markets, but few with access to the nearby Australian Stock Exchange where cash equities were traded. The lack of cross-fertilization certainly hampered the initial development of the market during the 1990s. Essentially, market-makers in equity derivatives products need access to the underlying cash market on the same terms as other players. For instance, during the 1980s, London's system of inter-dealer broker screens were only available to registered cash equity market-makers—thus placing integrated cash and options market-making firms at a potential advantage over the independent market-makers, who were not always able to access the stock market on such favourable terms. Similarly, with SSFs being largely ignored by the cash equity market-making community, the competitiveness of the product was essentially stunted in the Australian market and in similar markets.

Nowadays, the best equity market-makers have access to derivative products, although it is fairly frightening to note how many cash equity market-makers still rely on rather Dickensian processes, without recourse to modern products to help make them money—and indeed provide a better service for the equity investor. In that respect, the growth of SSFs can be a great thing for all investors, even if they never have direct exposure to the SSF marketplace themselves.

In the European equity options marketplace, it is interesting to note that some markets are much more developed relative to their cash market size than others. In Paris, for instance, and Amsterdam, a series of committed market-makers have subsequently exported their talents to the world.

However, liquidity isn't just about the liquidity providers, it also requires end-users; and in that respect it is interesting to note the extent to which SSF markets have already developed. While contract sizes are of a size to attract retail investors, most evidence suggests that SSFs traders are predominantly professional and institutional traders. There remains the key issue of whether or not the retail segment will actually endorse SSFs. True, there are the advantages (admittedly with concomitant dangers) of leverage, but equally the product has great flexibility, which ought to appeal to the retail user. However, it may take some time before SSFs gain widespread support among the retail investor fraternity. This is because of the need for retail investors to be educated about SSFs and the consequent delay before they are sufficiently up to speed to enter the market. Overall, numbers of retail futures traders are difficult to judge, although worldwide they probably total less than 500,000. Options traders probably number many times this figure, although those who are active may not significantly exceed the number of active retail futures traders by a factor of more than 2 or 3 at most. In any case, the likelihood is that it may take a year or two to really start to see a serious impact on the SSF marketplace from retail investors. Having said that, presuming sufficient liquidity, retail investors who are in the market earlier will garner significant insights into how best to trade SSFs to maximize their returns.

Of course, one of the key issues for retail investors is that SSFs don't just provide great speculative opportunities, they also provide considerable chances to hedge and indeed modify portfolio returns over short-term time periods, without necessarily having to actually sell out of core share positions.

HEDGING

In terms of simple hedging procedure, all user groups have the same opportunity to utilize SSFs.

Interpolated hedge

The interpolated hedge is a strategy that can be deployed by investors (or funds) who wish to invest sums of money in the market that they may not have yet received in total. For example, a pension fund may know it will receive another sum (say a million dollars) in a month's time from a new client and use cash in its current account to invest on margin in SSFs, thus giving it the alpha (absolute exposure) to the stock market ahead of actually receiving the money. Similarly, a retail investor can use SSFs to buy ahead of an event where they know more money will reach their investment account (e.g., a payment of a bonus or funds from a property they have sold, which will not be settled for a month). Therefore, with an interpolated hedge, SSFs can be an ideal means to gain specific stock exposure ahead of the full monies actually being received by an investor. Once the money is received, the investor can simultaneously sell their SSF position and buy the stock (usually as part of a single transaction on most electronic platforms) to eliminate basis risk.

Classic hedging

The aim of what we refer to as a classic hedge is to basically cover the downside risk in a marketplace. It can be employed by any form of investor, and indeed can be done fairly cost-effectively by retail investors given the relatively accessible size of most SSFs contracts. By using hedging strategies, funds or investors can protect themselves against downside risk. Selling SSFs provides the simplest way to cover exposure to a stock, or series of stocks. Of course, such hedges are most usually a direct hedge, in the form of a portfolio that contains, say, Microsoft stock and where the portfolio manager sells futures against that cash position to neutralize the market orientation. This may be for a very short period of time or during some particular event during which the manager expects the share to perform badly. Of course, the portfolio manager can "underhedge" his holding to reduce his upside gains, but leave himself open to some downside risk, instead of a pure hedge where effectively all risk and upside gain is negated. Likewise, if a fund manager wants to be short term short of a stock in his portfolio, he may choose to sell more futures than correlates directly with his portfolio and therefore have a net short exposure to the stock even if he holds a stash of the underlying cash. The good thing about SSFs is that even for managers with large blocks of a stock that they may not wish to dispose of, as they form a core portfolio-holding, there is always the opportunity to hedge against this holding using SSFs in a simple, cheap, and efficient fashion.

MARKET-MAKERS

Moving back to the liquidity argument, we find an interesting issue within the market-making realm (the methods of market-making are of course many and varied). The simplest form of market-making is based around the "edge" and making a price that effectively straddles value. In other words, the market-maker has a bid at, say, 38 and an offer at 40 (with "fair value" perceived at 39) and the market-maker hopes to buy at 38 and sell at 40 for a modest return.

Of course, in part the nature of market-making depends on how the market-making system itself operates and just how privileged the market-maker is in the exchange environment.

However, market-makers with access to the underlying cash market can provide a whole new dimension for market-making. True, when it comes to market-making in equity products, I suppose we all tend to harbour the same view of a classic "jobber" buying low, selling high, and exploiting the spread, whether through pure capitalism in open markets or through the privilege of being the exclusive conduit to matching, as is the case on many exchanges.

With SSFs, it is certainly true that a great many markets are being made by local capital and that they work assiduously to enhance liquidity, while all the time obviously bearing principal risk. Yet, in reality, there is already a hardy band of market-makers who are really camouflaged repo practitioners.

Repo is short for "repurchase", originally a bond market process where a holder of a security could make a sale in the spot market and simultaneously repurchase the same security at a forward date for a pre-agreed price. Essentially, all repurchase agreements work on a similar basis. In the equity market, repo trades have become increasingly common in certain circumstances.

The ability to short cash stock can vary considerably from jurisdiction to jurisdiction. The US and British markets lead the way in terms of simplicity, while France and Germany are overall pretty good. Spain pips Italy, which is probably the least stock borrower-friendly of the major European stock markets. Nevertheless, there are pockets of difficult-to-borrow stocks in several European jurisdictions. This is where the repo-trader can handily step in and securitize what is otherwise a market-making situation.

In the case of a difficult-to-borrow stock, the market-maker will therefore be left with a long futures position (as the counterparty obviously wants the short stock futures position) and needs to be able to short the stock. So, the way to efficiently make a market for the end-user in SSFs is to effectively make a price that relates to the repo cost of the trade, and, hey presto, the market-maker has completed a repo trade, while the end-user goes away happy with his short position.

Among the problems faced by short-sellers in cash markets, the obvious place to start is the ability to access the cash market to sell short in the first place. Locating parcels of borrowable stock can also pose problems. Moreover, stock that is borrowable may not be suitably "stable" (i.e., not prone to being called prior to the end of the trader's desired short-trading period). So, by building the stock-lending fee into the price, a repo-based market-maker can add liquidity, while himself running much lower risk on a trade than principal traders.

Likewise, the reduced risk to the marketplace can arguably be better for end-users, as they are not so reliant on what may be a relatively vague algorithm/relationship provided by "proprietary" market-makers—particularly where there are only one or two people making that market in any stock future. That's not to deprecate the abilities of the proprietary trading market-maker, but the "repo model" shows what can be done to allow an effectively guaranteed profit to a market-maker, while a narrow bid–offer spread ought to be a regular by-product of the stock-lending fee being built into the price.

However, repo market-makers do find themselves in a somewhat seasonal marketplace. Obviously, there are two quiet seasons when they can go about their market-making business without any unpleasant surprises. On the other hand, when it comes to the dividend season, suddenly a degree of uncertainty enters the transaction. First, the timing of the dividend is obviously key. As long as it falls within a particular contract month, there's really no particularly great impact on the repo market-maker. However, if the ex-dividend date is precariously close to the rollover date of contracts, then this can have a significant impact on the repo market-maker's relative certainty, which is built into their simple stock-lending fee model. Second, the size of the dividend is pretty critical too! So, during the dividend season, the repo market-maker has to contend with much more doubt and uncertainty. In some ways, being very close to the stock in question can be a great boon in trying to ascertain just when the ex-dividend date will fall as well as providing better data about what the dividend amount may be. In other words, a company with a significant local footprint may be better tuned into local market practice to estimate more accurately what the date and size of payments will be.

One intriguing aspect to the nascent, international SSFs trading business is that it provides a unique facility for traders to have easy access to shorting stock in markets that they have traditionally found difficult to access, let alone borrow stock in. This is therefore helping fuel hybrid market-making models, and indeed there would seem to be growing evidence that traders may be creating their own hybrid trades. For instance, for relative value ("pairs") transactions, some traders seem happy to buy cash equity in their local market, while the overseas (or local, but difficult to borrow) stock they seek to sell will be transacted through a short futures transaction.

SSFs truly are a cheap, simple, and efficient solution to many aspects of equity-trading, but their capacity to create a whole new dimension in the stock-trading revolution is growing all the time. The more and increasingly innovative the methods employed to make markets, the tighter the spreads and the more liquid the product, which will invariably not only benefit the end-user in stock futures but it will feed through to the speculators as well.

SPECULATORS

In the USA, SSFs have been saddled with high margins compared with many European markets (such as Euronext LIFFE and MEFF). Nevertheless, even at a fairly whopping 20%, the US stock speculator has a unique new tool to ply his trade at NQLX and OneChicago. With cash stock margin at 50%, the opportunity is still considerable, even at 20%. Similarly, the absence of the uptick rule in SSFs, means that potential short-sellers can easily sell short without being encumbered by waiting for an uptick.

Another key advantage for prospective sellers of a stock is that SSFs do not require any stock-borrowing, especially important as some very large corporations can be difficult to borrow stock in. For short-sellers, borrowing stock can be a real problem. With SSFs, there is no longer a problem in borrowing the stock, no matter how tightly held it may be. That is not merely a great boon to the speculator, it can also make the underlying stock more liquid to trade, because prospective short positions are less likely to be squeezed to extreme levels.

Of course, the biggest issue (which will take some time to resolve) will be whether the many options traders who utilize the likes of the CBOE with the aim of having a relatively "cheap" geared punt in markets will opt to move to

SSFs instead. Moreover, with the premium to SSFs being much smaller than the time value in an option, many speculators may prefer the relative simplicity of SSFs over the greater (or at least more management-intensive) risk of time value decay.

Nevertheless, as a speculative tool, there are few more cash-efficient instruments than straight futures, and even with the relatively high margins applied in the USA the possibilities for speculators are considerable. Of course, the speculators' trading strategies will be relatively simple, either seeking to buy or sell outright for the maximum potential profit.

FUND MANAGERS

We have already outlined how fund managers can employ hedging and interpolated hedging strategies to benefit their portfolio-positioning. Nevertheless, SSFs have a vast array of advantages for fund managers. True, fund managers may initially find the relative narrowness of the SSFs product range a disadvantage, because big funds may often hold more than 100 stocks. However, as liquidity has increased, so the breadth of product range has consistently improved ever since LIFFE and MEFF really kicked the SSF revolution off in 2000.

Of course UK fund managers (as well as individual investors) also have the unique advantage that SSFs can save them stamp duty. Lest you might have forgotten, stamp duty is a peculiarly British regressive tax on share-dealing (although various European and other countries apply stamp duties to other transactions, Britain is unique in applying it to share trades). On the other hand, at the time of writing, UK fund managers (and indeed hedge fund managers) have the advantage that they can use Over The Counter (OTC) traded Contracts For Difference (CFDs), which can provide even lower levels of margin than European SSFs—and consequently are often preferred to SSFs positions.

Equally, when it comes to fine-tuning cash flow within large fund portfolios, SSFs can be very beneficial where funds may be continually subject to redemptions and other cash adjustment. By judiciously employing SSFs, alpha returns can be maximized on a cash-effective basis, and the relative liquidity of SSFs permits traders to exit the market as and when they need to trim their positions.

Another interesting issue with SSFs is how the product also changes some almost fundamental tenets of portfolio management. For instance, by changing how securities-lending revenue can be taxed, by means of judicious use of SSFs in repo transactions to basically move that securities-lending revenue above the line so that it comes into the portfolio's core return, as opposed to being merely "other income".

Fund managers do have their gripes about SSFs. For one thing, the contract sizes are often viewed as being too small. Many fund managers therefore prefer large-scale cheaper dealing offered by OTC products, such as equity swaps and CFDs. Similarly, institutional managers often complain about the relatively disparate prices at which orders can be filled on fast-moving futures markets, preferring the homogeneous fills potentially provided by OTC products.

The narrow-based indices now growing as a sister product to SSFs have many advantages for the fund manager and can be a very useful conduit to helping manage risk in an environment where one or two shares in a sector may get very overvalued (or become undervalued) compared with the rest of the sector. While indexation may help create more and more Exchange Traded Funds which we expect to see dwarf "passive managed" funds over time, the opportunity to overlay narrow-based index futures with a multiplicity of cash and futures strategies will be a fascinating development, helping fund managers modify their portfolios to get the exposure they desire more easily while endlessly seeking to improve on their alpha.

On the other hand, some fund managers already have an issue with SSFs, because they have traditionally profited from placing pools of their stock in stock-lending positions and garnered an extra income from their holdings. In many respects, this is one bastion of opposition to SSFs that is going to be difficult to break down rapidly, although ultimately, as SSFs permit more tightly held stocks (or other shares where stock is difficult to borrow for whatever reason), the improved transparency of the equity market ought to make it a more reasonably valued place. Of course, speculative manias will continue to happen, crowd theory will remain a key facet to the trading game regardless of what happens with derivative and indeed cash products.

HEDGE FUNDS

Hedge fund managers are a slightly different breed to conventional fund managers, and for them SSFs are an ideal vehicle. However, there remain potential impediments to their using SSFs on a wide scale. For one thing, many hedge funds like to be very radically geared and, to this end, some were initially reluctant to enter the US SSFs market with 20% margins. Indeed, even in Europe, funds have been reluctant to use SSFs with much lower margins (in the 7.5–10% range) when they could achieve similar positions in the OTC market, where they may not have had to pay any margin at all in equity swaps, while in the CFD market margins, to suitably qualified institutions, can be a fraction even of existing European SSF margins. Nevertheless, the opportunity to create geared pairs trades so cheaply through SSFs is a major benefit for those pursuing aims close to the original models of hedge funds (such as those pioneered by Alfred Winslow Jones, with balanced long/short positions hedged for relative outperformance trades). Judicious use of narrow-based indices and SSFs provide for a heady mix of possible outcomes for the creative fund manager.

One lovely aspect of SSFs is the ease with which they can be administrated. No custodian relationships are required and the overall administration process in an ostensibly real-time clearing-and-settlement environment. Ultimately, as we discuss in the next section, risk transfer is becoming a key issue in all financial markets and, to this end, the core Central Counterparty Processing (CCP) advantages coupled with transparent dealing on SSFs is a great advantage for the future of the product.

RISK TRANSFER

Aside from all that juicy speculation out there in financial markets, the issue of risk transfer has of course long been a focal point of the derivatives business. Of late, various innovations such as Basle 2 and a host of national regulatory measures have gradually been trying to push trading off OTC and onto exchanges. For instance, in late 2002, the EU Undertakings for Collective Investment in Transferable Securities (UCITS) guidelines were further beefed up with a view to controlling risk on OTC instruments by pension fund, unit trust, and mutual fund investors. Given that the issue of meeting pensions obligations for investors remains pivotal for the governments of all the world's major economies, the issue of ensuring probity in investment will similarly become increasingly important during this decade. This is a boon for all exchange-traded products and indeed specifically for SSFs.

Of course, the whole question of just what is a fair balance in risk management terms for OTC products remains one of the most emotionally charged issues in financial markets. Banks want to retain an adults-only marketplace for their own dealings, and indeed it is difficult to argue that consenting adult institutions ought to be allowed to do their own thing in private ... although, given that adult club members have included the likes of Barings Bank, BCCI, and so forth, one is inclined to be a tad concerned about counterparty risk even if only as a retail banking customer! Then again, as the sage folk would note, while the likes of collapsed hedge fund LTCM threatened to rip a whole in the world's banking balance sheets when it collapsed, the (admittedly less expensive) demise of Barings through on-exchange transactions made barely a ripple by comparison in financial markets, thanks to Nick Leeson's foibles being entirely on-exchange and therefore CCP-cleared.

Perhaps one of the more interesting issues is how the measures seek to restrict counterparty risk on portfolios so that only between 5 and 10% of assets in any person's pension scheme are held by one counterparty. Similarly, the guidelines are concerned with the spread of risk that would affect anybody holding, for instance, the bonds, warrants, and cash equity of a particular single company. However, it is perhaps the counterparty risk issue which could become the most significant for OTC equity derivatives markets, and this is ultimately likely to benefit the SSFs environment. The issue with CFDs, for instance, is a key one, as pension fund managers may need to split their holdings across multiple managers, whereas they can deal more flexibly via the exchange and clearing house for SSFs. Naturally, the sheer logistics alone of holding multiple CFD positions with different brokers may prove to be an irritant to the pension funds, presumably leading to greater exchange trade. In particular, whereas SSF positions can in fact be executed through any broker on an exchange such as NQLX or OneChicago, CFDs need to be executed through the broker with whom they were first opened to ensure offset and closure of existing positions.

True, the overall impact of the UCITS guidelines won't affect the ordinary account holders in CFDs, but such moves will push liquidity toward the exchanges if institutions find it more economical to deal through these markets. The economic advantages for trading in the leading SSFs will doubtless start to win over business from the OTC providers. Nevertheless, the flexibility of CFDs in providing access to a wider range of stocks not already listed on exchanges will remain.

Another aspect in the overall risk transfer issue is of course inextricably linked with CCP. However, regulators are now beginning to tighten up, and in this respect it is pension fund managers and trustees who can find themselves at risk if they make an oversight. For instance, the movement for trustees to be responsible for scrutinizing every counterparty in a pension fund portfolio is gaining pace, especially within Europe. In this respect, suddenly the merits of CCP are becoming a great deal more transparent to many trustees who don't wish to run the risk of seeing a supposedly solid counterparty biodegrade. In this respect, once again the advantage appears to lie solidly with SSFs products as opposed to their OTC cousins.

Overall, as more regulations are likely to encourage the use of exchanges for various reasons, it would seem safe to presume that this will be to the advantage of all investors seeking sound risk transfer, hedging, and speculative opportunities in equity markets through SSFs.

HYBRID MARKET-MAKING

We mentioned above how market-making for all products can be enhanced by SSFs, and indeed the fundamental interconnectedness of financial products means that the opportunities to offset risks through different instruments now abound. Likewise, they can permit more and more permutations for market-making. For instance, the process of simple cash equity market making can potentially be enhanced and tightened by accessing SSFs as an offset.

Likewise, there can be many advantages to using futures to make markets, even as a substitute to cash, in cash-settled options. Take, for instance, the issue of options positions that have a net long market direction (positive delta). To delta-hedge and basically strip out the directional bias so as to be left trading only volatility, the market-maker must sell stock short. This usually entails borrowing stock to cover short stock held against most options positions. On the other hand, the possibility remains to employ SSFs as a substitute for cash equities in such market-making. Naturally, as SSFs can be sold as easily as they can be bought, this makes life a lot easier for the market-maker and removes any potential hassle (with the uptick rule, for instance). However, it then also leads us into a whole fascinating new world (beyond the scope of this book, which is trying to avoid too many tricky sums!), where the market-makers can each make a "fair value" using different instruments to hedge (i.e., cash or futures), and this can result in the possibility of an arbitrage for others in the difference between the market-makers' prices ... Of course this arbitrage only further adds to liquidity, which is very handy for one and all seeking to trade the product.

In various markets for instance, there have been many cash-settled index options that have been traditionally priced off the back of the futures, thus introducing an infinitesimal disparity in pricing. More widespread usage of SSFs as a vehicle for hedging underlying equity options that deliver/settle to the cash price is highly likely to create the same effect. Of course such keen observers of these forms of arbitrage will also be the ones who seek to strip and modify narrow-based indices to their own liking by adding in other stocks or removing key stocks through selling SSFs against their core narrow-index holdings. Similarly, we expect to see SSFs play a greater role not merely in individual equity option market-making but perhaps also being used to offset certain warrant market exposures as well.

> Derivatives markets are finally coming of age, and these products
> might help to bridge the gap between derivatives and cash investors.
>
> Diane Garnick (2002)

ANOTHER WEAPON FOR PROGRAM-TRADING

Program-trading is perhaps one of the most talked about and equally most misunderstood facets of contemporary financial markets. Very simply, program-trading in its purest form relates to trading on the basis of a basket of cash equities against a futures index.

The Greek letter beta (β) is used in financial markets to denote the sensitivity of a particular share to an index. By combining a basket of stocks, index arbitrageurs can manage to replicate an index and thus indulge in the fine art of program-trading. A program trade involves trading the differential in the cash index and the premium (or discount) of the index future.

Essentially, thanks to the impact of dividends and the cost of financing positions, etc., there is always a relative difference between a futures index (which will expire in some predetermined number of weeks or months) and a cash index (which is basically the value of stocks today). While there is a mathematical formula to assess fair value (the perceived equilibrium relationship between a cash index and an index future), the reality is that, thanks to all the outside influences to which markets are exposed, the actual fair value level is rarely the level at which a market actually trades. When the fair value level is exceeded by a certain amount (which itself depends on the disposition of the trader), program trades will be triggered with a view to profiting when the market returns to fair value. There are two core program trades:

(1)   When the premium on the futures index extends significantly above fair value: buy cash stock, sell index futures (aiming to see the premium reduce toward fair value).
(2)   When the premium on the cash index is below fair value (perhaps at a discount to the cash index): sell cash stock, buy index futures.

These basic program trades (known as "index arbitrage") are fairly simple to follow, but they amount to less than 10% of the daily program-trading activity.[1]

The thing to bear in mind is that program-trading is reputed to account for as much as 30% of US equity business. The business is predicated on a variety of spread trades covering the relationship between cash equities and futures indices. With the advent of SSFs, now you can even try to employ them to fine-tune index arbitrage strategies.

ISLAMIC FINANCE

One particularly interesting element of SSFs is that they can be applied to Islamic finance in a way that dividend-paying (and therefore non-Islamic, as usury is banned) cash shares cannot. Essentially, the pure capital gain component of SSFs makes them appealing to practitioners of Islamic

---

[1] Source: HL Camp & Company, http://www.programtrading.com/faq.htm

finance, which is gaining increasing popularity throughout the Islamic world and indeed even with non-Muslims in the Middle East.

STOCK LENDERS

We mentioned above how many institutions have lent stock via stock-lending agencies to allow short-sellers to sell stock short. Their business is undoubtedly the most likely to be affected by a major growth in SSFs business. That said, they may retain a niche if such products as CFDs continue to prosper (as we expect they will).

CFDs may not be as transparent and readily tradable as SSFs in many respects, but they are more flexible in being able to provide access to stocks that may be too small to be readily listed as an SSF in their own right. Similarly, there may yet be a market for some stock lenders in the physical delivery of SSFs, as some folk will borrow to cover short-term delivery liabilities, perhaps as part of a more complex strategy.

CASH EQUITY BROKERS

Here we plunge into the great unknown. It is no exaggeration to state that cash equity brokers are fundamentally a conservative breed. However, will they adjust to the new reality of a world with SSFs or simply seek to keep peddling cash products? The omens from historical analysis (over the past 30 years) are probably discouraging, despite the fact that SSFs provide such a beneficial overlap to cash equity markets. Nevertheless, we expect SSFs to remain something provided by a predominantly specialist derivatives broker community, despite the fact that many more people could benefit from them. Alas, perceptions about the casino-like nature of futures-trading remain, and, certainly in the USA, there remains much work to be done if futures contracts can genuinely get some way closer to the mainstream of financial market activity. Similarly, there is always the issue of whether the growth in SSFs might put brokers out of business. In this case, we doubt it. Indeed, the evidence from all futures contracts in the past has been that the launch of liquid futures contracts tends to make the underlying market more liquid and thus enhance volume in the cash market as well. In this case, the growth of SSFs ought to be an absolute boon to the cash brokerage community, even if they might opt (disappointingly) to shun the product in many instances.

WINNERS AND LOSERS

It is difficult to really identify any major losers in the equity trading community apart from stock lenders. Brokers can see their revenues increase, hedge fund and active fund managers can enhance their returns in a multiplicity of ways, and retail investors willing to endorse the product can also increase their opportunities not merely with additional directional risk (of course, short-selling now becomes much simpler) but also through the much easier methods of trading pairs and other spreads made possible by SSFs. Market-makers and creators of structured products already find a great benefit to be derived from SSFs, and those benefits filter through to all market users. In this respect, SSFs are certainly a win–win product for everybody in financial markets. Of course, the use of electronic trading, even in the USA, for SSFs may also refocus many priorities and ultimately cause certain arbitrage disparities to be more easily controlled and removed from the scene. However, with the likelihood of SSF expansion (rising from a mere couple of hundred underlying shares worldwide to perhaps 2,000 or more within three or four years), there are more than ample opportunities for further arbitrage as liquidity trickles down through later SSFs issues. Of course, the key for exchanges will be in trying to introduce SSFs that stoke the public imagination and attract recurring business on a regular basis. Not all SSFs trade every day, and indeed some only really attract strong volumes at certain cyclical phases (e.g., their results seasons, etc.). Nevertheless, in a world of scarce bandwidth resources, exchanges will need to choose carefully just which stocks to list, as there is going to be a finite pool of liquidity provision and indeed a fairly finite listing of SSFs for the foreseeable future—although that "finite" amount is likely to stretch to four figures.

6
Margin, Clearing, and Settlement

MARGIN

Margin is of course a key facet to all forms of derivatives-trading. A deposit is paid by both buyer and seller (initial margin) when they enter a position and a running total is kept by marking the position to market, which along with other types of "variation" margin ensures that the clearing house (which matches every buyer to every seller) can keep risks managed effectively. Of course, the benefit to the counterparties are several:

(a)   futures are a very cash-effective means of trading in financial markets;
(b)   spread traders and hedgers can use other assets to offset their positions through netting;
(c)   the integrity of the clearing house means that counterparty risk is effectively eradicated.

Of course, stocks have also been traded on a margined basis, particularly in the USA, for many years. Investors with a suitable margin account can leverage their positions, nowadays through a 50% down payment of the stock's value. In this respect, it is probably fair to say that the treatment of margin for cash equities compared with futures positions was a key factor in the long-standing debates about the Shad–Johnson Accord, which effectively legitimized US single stock options, but outlawed Single Stock Futures (SSFs). Ultimately, the Securities and Exchange Commission's (SEC) long regulatory history dates back to the aftermath of the crash of 1929 and the subsequent crushing bear market. This produced a relative flurry of legislation by the Roosevelt Administration, designed to restore confidence in financial institutions. The Securities

Act of 1933 was aimed at enforcing fuller disclosure about new issues of securities and the accountability of issuers and investment bankers. The Glass—Steagall Act of 1933 separated investment-banking from commercial banking and introduced deposit insurance. The Securities Exchange Act 1934 created the SEC. One of the SEC's core mandates on its foundation in 1934 was to look at both short-selling and indeed margin-trading. Before the crash there was evidence of some very low stock margins being paid, and indeed this process was effectively throttled after 1929. Regulatory fiat now imposes the 50% margin limit.

This is intriguing as margins for most futures contracts is vastly lower than this. In the bond and money markets it can be a mere 3–5% of the contract's underlying value. The SEC and its cash stock market constituency must have felt very uneasy about the prospects of SSFs having such low margin levels.

One key group in the stock futures arena who must have a degree of natural disinclination for this product are the margin and stock-lending organizations. These are invariably large, well-funded institutions that add to returns. Effectively, stock-lending is a small industry (small in number, but hardly a cottage industry), with a value estimated at over $500 million on the NYSE/NASDAQ alone in 2001) compared with the overall stock market, but it is nonetheless a lucrative and influential one on Wall Street and in other financial centres.

Cash single stock margins are set at 50% for buying stock and 150% for sellers of stock (i.e., sellers do not receive the consideration received for the stock sold and pay a 50% margin against their position). If one starts to multiply these margins by even the lowest of interest rates, suddenly it becomes clear that the take in terms of interest income alone for the stock-lending industry is considerable. In the same time-honoured fashion that turkeys tend to abstain from voting for Thanksgiving or Christmas (depending on their birthplace either side of the Atlantic), it is not unreasonable to presume that the stock-lending industry has a marked reluctance to suddenly lose this wonderfully lucrative float of cash (even when Alan Greenspan was setting interest rates appreciably proximate to zero during 2002).

When it came to establishing SSFs, the derivatives industry fought a concerted campaign to try and set these margin levels as low as possible. The levels initially discussed in the USA suggested initial margins of 25–30%. In the final reckoning, the US SSFs market launched with minimum initial margins of 20% for shorts and longs. Obviously, this represented a major victory for the futures industry, but even so the margin levels are still somewhat giddy compared with the circa 7–8% levels typically seen in the European markets for SSFs. Initially, LIFFE expected margins to be set at around 7.5–10% in their initial discussion documents, but, despite the substantial post-dotcom collapse volatility of the stock market during 2001 and 2002, the London Clearing House (LCH) has been able to maintain margins around these levels (if not slightly lower rates than this expectation). Of course, margin is always changing in precise percentage terms as price changes, and indeed, when some stocks hit huge volatility, margins can go up (variation margin calls can be made intraday when the marketplace gets particularly volatile, for instance). Therefore, while most LIFFE Universal Stock Futures (USFs) margins in late 2002 were around the 7–8% level, Swisscom was as low as 4.1%, while the rather more volatile Ericsson was at one stage as high as 58%! In this respect, margin always reflects the degree of risk in a stock, based on relatively recent price history.

Of course, these margin levels are the lowest set rates and most clients will pay a higher rate. The clearing house dictates what the minimum margin is, and then it is up to the broker to decide how to margin their clients. In practice, retail investors may pay at least double margins in many cases, which reflects the relative risk of the small trader compared with the massive leviathans of finance, such as the bulge bracket banks.[1] Indeed, it is within the bulge bracket banks that the biggest issues arise for minimum margin levels. After all, despite innovations such as the Basle treaties on banking capital adequacy and the Over The Counter (OTC)[2] market, the big banks can basically trade bilaterally with other major banks and not have to pay a cent in margin. This is where the minimum margin issue becomes key. Banks are in the business of managing their capital as best they can, and therefore leveraging their assets is a very vital facet of their business model. When faced with two similar products that can provide essentially similar returns where one requires a 20% margin and the other requires none, it doesn't really require a doctorate in Mathematics to see which one the banker is likely to prefer. Indeed, in the UK and Europe, the very low margin rates for contracts for difference often encourage OTC-literate players such as hedge funds to take stock exposure there with initial margins as low as 1.5% on occasions.

Leaving aside the issue of just how margins that are cheaper (or zero) can be more attractive to major institutions, a very important issue to bear in mind is of course how this fragments and ultimately harms the marketplace as such. As Patrick Young (2003) has discussed in *New Capital Market Revolution* in many respects the established exchange-trading business is an absolute minnow compared with its OTC cousin. Now, of course, the fact that much of the business is transacted OTC has an impact not merely on liquidity in exchanges but also on the total transparency of the marketplace. Similarly,

---

[1] Bulge bracket banks are those regarded as being among the elite of Wall Street and the global investment and retail banking markets.

[2] This is the "upstairs" market in sophisticated commodity, money market, and equity products, and is not to be confused with the OTC stock markets that have been tainted by "boiler room" accusations, etc. in past decades.

the issue of market integrity is key. Although it rarely happens, financial institutions can hit hard times, and the history of financial markets is littered with financial disasters that have seen the closure or near destruction of many financial empires. In the OTC market, the knock-on effects can be considerable. Indeed, the LTCM (Long-Term Credit Management) hedge fund collapse in 1998 nearly had a phenomenal impact on all financial markets. Where business is transacted on exchanges, the difference is that the risk is being measured by a clearing house, which has a much clearer picture of the holistic market position. In this respect, ironically, higher initial margins can actually endanger the financial system. By protecting the stock-lending business through setting artificially high SSFs margin levels, the effect is actually to discourage institutions from trading on exchanges and, in addition to reducing potential liquidity, it also results in the risk being taken to OTC markets, where it is more difficult to manage and account for. Hence, high margins, somewhat counter-intuitively, encourage greater systemic risk ... Hardly a sensible move in an era where central bankers are always harping on about the need for increased transparency of risks ...

Indeed, the US Federal Reserve and US Treasury were felt to have exerted influence behind the scenes to try and get US SSF margins reduced to as "low" as 20% for shorts and longs. Of course, the history of these special margin requirements date back to the amendments by Congress in December 2000 (the Commodity Futures Modernization Act) to permit the trading of SSFs contracts and futures on narrow-based stock indices ("security futures"). This legislation, which essentially serves two masters, the stock market regulator of the SEC and the futures markets regulatory body, the Commodity Futures Trading Commission (CFTC) (see p. 11), means that there are some differences in the treatment of SSFs for different market participants that impact upon their particular margin, clearing, and settlement regimes, because these contracts are effectively regulated simultaneously as both securities products and futures products, depending on your business's core orientation. Therefore, those who carrying customer security futures accounts have to be registered with the SEC as broker–dealers as well as with the CFTC as Futures Commission Merchants (FCMs). In addition, with a series of core regulations adopted by both the SEC and the CFTC, broker–dealer/FCMs who trade security futures on behalf of customers are required to comply with special margin requirements for these products ("margin rules").

These margin rules are based upon Federal Reserve Board Regulation T (which is the core regulation that establishes margin requirements for stocks and bonds, cash, or futures). Applied to SSFs, the Regulation T rules have been adapted to reflect the special attributes of security futures. As a result, the applicability of the margin rules differs in some cases depending on whether a trade or position is carried in a securities account or a futures account. So if your account is with an FCM who is only regulated by the CFTC and your trades are in a commodity/futures account, you may not benefit by offsetting any SEC-regulated instruments. However, if your FCM is regulated by both authorities and you wish to benefit by offsetting, then placing all trades in a securities account would appear to be the best answer.

In terms of practical application in the USA, there are reductions in margins for various strategies:

- Calendar spreads. Reflecting on the fact that a calendar spread involves buying (selling) a near month and selling (buying) a month further away from expiration, the net exposure to the market is much less. In fact, it is really limited to only the difference between the two legs of the position on the day the near month leg expires. Once the near leg expires, the position (if held) becomes a simple long/short futures position and is margined as such. However, as a spread, the calendar spread attracts a minimum initial maintenance of 5%, applied to whichever leg is the greater price (i.e., the larger margin) between the long and short components.
- Collars. A collar involves SSFs and options all together. Essentially, the position is one in which the holder is long the SSF, long the puts (at a lower strike price) and long calls (at a higher strike price) on the same security. In other words, the position involves holding an options strangle with a long future. The minimum margin is the lesser of: (a) 10% of the aggregate exercise price of the put plus the aggregate put out-of-the-money amount; or (b) 20% of the aggregate exercise price of the call plus the aggregate call in-the-money amount.
- With a hedged position where the customer is long or short an SSF and short or long the underlying security, then margin is 5% of the position with the greater market value. Effectively, here the client is only trading the premium relationship in the stock against the future, so the total risk is significantly reduced, similar to the calendar spread (hence the much lower margin).

For positions that are market-neutral and involve a combination of SSFs and stock options (e.g., conversions and reverse conversions), then the minimum margin is set at 10% of the aggregate exercise price of the options plus the in-the-money amount of the short option. As we discussed earlier, a conversion involves selling a call and buying a put at the same strike and then buying the SSF (of course, one can also buy the cash equity for this trade). A reversal (or reverse conversion) involves buying a call and selling a put at the same strike while selling the future. The end result is a trade that is directionally- and volatility-neutral:

- If you hold a long position in an instrument that is convertible into the underlying security (e.g., convertible bonds), then these securities can be deposited as collateral with the clearing house in order to attract a margin against a SSFs futures position of 10% of the market valuation of the convertible security.

• When it comes to narrow-based indices, margins are reduced when you replicate the futures index using SSFs. In other words, arbitrageurs or spread-traders seeking to trade the relationship between the index components and the overall index value pay only 5% of the value of the higher valued position (long or short leg). Naturally, the SSF components of the narrow-based index must be with precisely the same shares and in exact proportion to the index against which the spread is made. (On a similar note, where there is a spread between a future on a broad-based stock index, you can deploy a basket of narrow-based index futures based on and in the exact same proportion to the securities underlying the broad-based index to trade this spread too.) The minimum initial maintenance margin is once again 5% of the current market valuation of the basket of SSFs.

However, here is the rub: these strategies only receive the above margin treatment if they are held in a security account, not a futures account. In other words, they fall under the remit of the SEC and not the CFTC.

While it is usual to talk about cash margin levels, in fact a series of different instruments can be deployed in margin accounts (securities or futures). Regulation T stipulates a list of acceptable "margin securities", which basically includes equity securities traded on a recognized US exchange or NASDAQ. Also acceptable is any debt security, as well as certain OTC and foreign securities, mutual fund shares, and debt securities that are convertible into margin-eligible securities, as well as exempted securities (including US government, agency, and municipal debt—from Treasury Bills to bonds and indeed GNMAs [Government National Mortgage Associations).

Incidentally, SSFs themselves are not eligible as margin collateral, but "free equity" including unrealized profit could be used as margin—although some brokers may not permit this (again it all depends on your credit-rating: institutions usually can, private individuals often cannot).

Letters of credit have been specifically excluded as collateral for margin with SSFs. Money market mutual fund shares may be accepted, but only if there is a tripartite agreement between the broker–dealer/FCM, the customer, and the money market fund manager or its transfer agent that allows for the shares to be redeemed if necessary in a speedy fashion. Essentially, a key rule of margin collateral remains that clearing agents and clearing houses like any security that can be readily converted into cash. In this respect, bearer securities such as bonds and bills are very popular! The problem with money market mutual funds is that unless they can be sold quickly and without recourse to the holder, the clearing agent/house has a risk they need to cover. For instance, if the account holder died, transfer may be difficult, or if he or she simply refused to sanction a transfer, this still has the effect of transferring the risk to the clearing house.

Much of the futures marketplace works on a system of risk-based portfolio-margining, known as Standard Portfolio Analysis of Risk (SPAN). In 1988, the CME developed and implemented the SPAN system for calculating performance bond requirements. SPAN was the first futures industry performance bond system ever to calculate requirements exclusively on the basis of overall portfolio risk. In the years since its inception, SPAN has become the industry standard; the program is now the official performance bond mechanism of virtually every registered futures exchange and clearing organization in the USA, as well as many such entities worldwide. The objective of SPAN is to identify overall risk in a complete portfolio of futures and options derivative instruments. The program treats futures and options uniformly, while at the same time recognizing the unique exposures associated with options portfolios. In addition, the program recognizes both inter-month and inter-commodity risk relationships. So it basically takes a holistic view of the entire risk profile held by a client. In other words, there can be allowances if, for instance, the holder is long on bonds and short on bills, as they have ostensibly similar risk profiles.

However, with SSFs this is not going to be applied, which means that SSFs will be margined independently. Naturally, this ought to ensure that higher margins are paid by end-users, which is good in terms of managing risks but also concomitantly bad for exchange usage and overall transparency, as it may fail to encourage OTC users to abandon their CFDs and equity swaps for exchange products, because once again it confers a potential margin disadvantage on SSFs.

While the US markets do not have SPAN-margining, the system has been applied to USFs at LIFFE since their launch in January 2001. Similarly, SPAN is employed by BVLP in Portugal, Spain's MEFF, and the Indian NSE.

While margins are not fixed and each clearing house makes its decisions in isolation concerning margin rates, the use of SPAN and other standard methodologies for assessing risk means that the overall margin rates tend to be in the region of 5–10% on the non-US exchanges. Of course, this raises the intriguing question of whether margin will ultimately be the key factor that helps kick-start liquidity? Certainly, from an OTC perspective, as we have already discussed, high margins are a major disincentive for OTC market players to remotely consider the various benefits of the exchange marketplace. All market players are price-sensitive, and, in a world with scarce resources, it is quite feasible that US SSFs may yet be overlooked as an investment class by traders who believe their capital can be better allocated to lower cost instruments. After all, it seems somewhat strange that the percentage margin on a stock index such as the S&P 500 is approximately 7%, while the margin on a narrow-based index is approximately 8%, yet to buy an SSF in the USA (which is a component of both the narrow-based index and the S&P 500) will require an initial 20% margin deposit! In many respects, America is the home of capitalism and drives the world's financial markets. Therefore, the US marketplace is likely to be pivotal in the development of SSFs as a core risk transfer and speculative instrument. The next few years may yet require some progress on margins if the product is going to achieve the ubiquity that it ought. On the other hand, if the US market opts against widespread adoption of margin rates, more in line with the world of derivatives *per se*, is there a prospect of overseas competition seeking to usurp the USA in its own products? Certainly, the imposition of withholding taxes and other regulatory impediments during the 1960s helped boost London as a financial centre, effectively gifting the Eurobond market to London from the US, for instance, when an American regulatory fiat clamped down on it. In the case of SSFs the picture looks slightly more confused. For one thing, the only non-US exchange offering US-based SSFs is LIFFE, and, while at the time of writing they continue to list contracts that can be traded, it would not be a great surprise if they are delisted soon. This would likely be a "political" considera-tion because of Euronext LIFFE's partnership with NASDAQ in the NQLX venture. There are arguments for allowing the contract to continue, if only because it is not inconceivable that some time in the future we will have parallel contracts that are cash-settled. There is a possibility that if US margins remained stubbornly high then NASDAQ and LIFFE might take a leaf out of the Swedish OM exchange's book[3] and offer the contracts once more via LIFFE Connect, in which case there would be order-routing already available from the NQLX to LIFFE Connect (albeit in a different city). Overall, it is difficult to see the other leading SSF markets, the Indian, Portu-guese, and Spanish exchanges—trying to enter the US marketplace ... although it would seem silly not to rule out an opportunistic attempt by a European exchange at some future juncture, as they would likely have little to lose.

Nevertheless, in the event that SSFs development is stunted or perceived to be stunted—by overly high margin rates, expect to see some interesting lateral developments in market structure during the course of the next few years—certainly after 2003—if the market is not showing encouraging growth signs.

---

[3] In the 1980s, the Swedish government introduced a withholding tax on Swedish government bonds and futures that led OM to establish a subsidiary exchange, OMLX (LX standing for London Exchange), based in the UK, which traded the same contracts as OM in Stockholm. Traders could opt to transact their business on OM Stockholm and be liable for withholding tax or direct their business to London and avoid the tax entirely. The Swedish government soon found itself forced to rescind the tax, as it wasn't raising revenue and was in fact endangering the Swedish financial markets that were gradually moving to London.

CLEARING, SETTLEMENT AND DELIVERY

Cash versus physical settlement

At the time of writing the Euronext LIFFE exchange almost exclusively lists cash-settled USFs, at the time of writing although it has considered adding physical delivery to all stocks on various occasions (including before launch in early 2001). In late November 2002, Euronext LIFFE did effectively change four Scandinavian stocks from cash settlement to physical delivery. Driven by demands in the most liquid—Nokia OYJ—the exchange also changed the delivery arrangements for its three other Scandinavian stocks, creating what have become known as physical delivery USFs: Danske Bank A/S, Novo Nordisk, and Norsk Hydro ASA. The reason for this was essentially that the Scandinavian markets settle daily on the last traded price, or a reference price. However, this price could vary from LIFFE's official settlement method, which is a Variable Weighted Average Price-based (VWAP) procedure, and in this case reflects business during the last 10 minutes of trade in a share. Of course, the Exchange Delivery Settlement Price (EDSP) on a cash-settled USF could therefore be significantly different from that of the daily last traded (official exchange settlement) price. Therefore, LIFFE took the initiative to change the settlement procedure to physical delivery and in so doing helped to alleviate the disparity, because any difference in the settlement price is carried into the cash that the settling trader either delivers or takes delivery of and they can then exit their cash position at the cash market price on the next trading day.

In Spain and Portugal, the MEFF and BVLP, respectively, permit traders to elect whether to take delivery or prefer cash settlement when they trade. Overall, physical settlement seems to have taken preference in these markets. The Indian market is also physically settled. Meanwhile in America, all SSFs are physically settled contracts. While it was too early in the SSFs development cycle to discern what sort of percentage of SSFs would be held to delivery, it is fair to say that physical delivery is a fairly marginal activity. In most commodity and financial futures markets where physical delivery takes place, it usually only occurs in a tiny percentage of cases—less than 1%. Interestingly, when LIFFE first listed SSFs there was a considerable process of discussion with interested parties, and, at the time, there was no consensus pushing for one mode of settlement over the other and ultimately LIFFE chose simplicity with cash settlement. As the SSFs market has developed and physical settlement has become more widespread, the popularity of physical settlement among end-users has increased. We examine the delivery process around the world for existing SSFs in the following section.

NQLX and OneChicago have decided to go with the Options Clearing Corporation (OCC) as their primary clearer. OneChicago also permits certain traders to clear through the CME clearing house (see below). OCC was founded in 1973 and is the central counterparty for all US equity options-trading. Under its SEC jurisdiction, OCC clears transactions for put and call options on common stocks and other equity issues, stock indexes, foreign currencies, interest rate composites, and SSFs. As a registered derivatives clearing organization (under CFTC jurisdiction), they provide settlement services for transactions in futures and options on futures. The OCC is owned jointly by the American Stock Exchange, Chicago Board Options Exchange, International Securities Exchange, Pacific Exchange, and the Phila-delphia Stock Exchange.

The National Securities Clearing Corporation (NSCC) is a wholly owned subsidiary of the Depository Trust & Clearing Corporation (DTCC), the major clearing and settlement agency for US equities.

Both OneChicago and NQLX have gone down the physical delivery route. This probably reflects a mixture of client demand and a natural American inclination toward ensuring physically deliverable contracts wherever possible. In political terms, it probably also helps ameliorate relations with the cash equity community, who at least feel there is more chance of delivery adding to underlying equity market volume as opposed to cash settlement, which in many ways disintermediates the underlying stock market from this process. Arguments abound on the merits of cash versus physical settlement, and it seems at the time of writing that the groundswell of user opinion is heading in favour of the physically deliverable route, although this is a fairly recent phenomenon. Naturally, arguments very strongly cited in favour of the physical delivery method include the key issue that physical settlement tends to alleviate any issues there may be with settlement prices in stocks on a particular expiry day (for whatever reason), etc. So, in the US market, the OCC clears all SSFs transactions and co-ordinates with the NSCC to effect delivery against the open positions. General Clearing Members (GCMs) must meet the various criteria of both the exchange and the OCC, in terms of capital adequacy and so forth, and are not only permitted to clear trades for their own accounts but also those of clients. Anybody wishing to trade on NQLX or OneChicago must use a GCM registered on that marketplace.

While in the broad sweep of things the delivery process of most exchanges is similar, whether by physical delivery or cash settlement, each exchange has its own very particular rules that cover local needs and conditions. Let's take the physical delivery rules first.

NQLX

NQLX has an advantage in that both LIFFE and NASDAQ come from a background where the use of technology is not new. LIFFE has for some years been screen-based through its LIFFE Connect^{TM} system. Since the inception of LIFFE in 1982 as a floor-based market, the exchange employed the computerized trade registration system.

However, working in the American context, LIFFE NASDAQ has often found itself dealing with organizations that are probably on a slightly steeper learning curve. The US markets remain predominantly open outcry at this juncture, and this means that technological deployment even in clearing and settlement may not be so advanced in many areas. Nevertheless, overall, clearers such as OCC do have considerable experience of automation processes through the options markets, in particular the ground-breaking US ISE, which grew at a fairly staggering pace against its open outcry opposition during its first years of operation. NQLX, like OneChicago, opted for physical delivery of its SSFs contracts.

GCMs have the ability to carry business in either security or futures accounts (depending on their regulatory status), but must be able to make delivery either directly or indirectly. To settle directly, the GCM must be a member of both the OCC and the NSCC. To settle indirectly, a GCM must be a member of the OCC and have an account with an NSCC member who will act as an agent for the GCM. In other words, indirect settlement means that the GCM will use a registered stockbroker to effect delivery—this is often the case, for instance, with GCMs who are based in the futures/options markets, but do not have a cash equity brokerage within their corporate umbrella.

The last trading day is the third Friday of the contract delivery month and trade closes at the usual time (4:02 p.m. EST [Eastern Standard Time]). Settlement for the delivery contract will, on this contract only, be calculated based on the closing prices of the underlying securities on their primary securities markets. EDSP will be used to make all calculations, with regards to the final settlement process.

OCC will receive all data from TRS as per usual on the final trading day. The GCM may make final adjustments to their gross positions until 08:00 p.m. EST that day using OCC's CMACS system.

OCC will generate two reports: one titled the "futures delivery advise report" and the other titled the "futures cash settlement report".

OCC will provide each GCM with a futures delivery advice report indicating the GCM's long and short positions in each expired SSF and the total delivery obligation. For GCMs who are not NSCC members, the OCC provides the report to the member of the NSCC with whom the GCM has an account. This report will also detail any special settlement procedures or circumstances—such as when a corporate event occurs that takes place at or near settlement.

The futures cash settlement report is generated to reflect any cash movement needed as a result of a corporate event.

The OCC sends a report at the end of the last trade day to the NSCC detailing all physical deliveries and all related payments that are due on the third business day after expiration ($T + 3$). Once this information has been transferred (which includes specifying which GCMs are making and taking delivery), the OCC's role in the delivery process is complete, although, of course, the OCC's primary activity remains all the daily central counterparty processing functions of a clearing house, such as matching every buyer to every seller and ensuring adequate margin collection, etc.

Meanwhile, the settlement process now resides with NSCC. On the first business day after expiration $(T+1)$, the NSCC initiates procedures for physical delivery of the securities underlying the SSFs using its Continuous Net Settlement (CNS) system. Through the CNS system, the NSCC reduces the transactions requiring physical delivery by netting each NSCC member's total buy obligation against its sell obligation and establishes one net position for each security. The same netting occurs for any cash settlements.

On the evening of the first business day after expiration, the NSCC provides each member with the results of these internally matched offsetting positions in a report called the "consolidated trade summary". Using the data from this report each NSCC member specifies how it intends to make or take delivery of the securities underlying the SSFs. Note that the NSCC member has two choices: to accept physical delivery of the securities or to internally match offsetting positions among its customers' accounts. At 11:59 p.m. EST on $T+1$ all secururities transactions that have been processed up to this point are guaranteed by the NSCC.

During the next business day $(T+2)$, NSCC members receive notice of their settlement obligation from the NSCC. The process of the physical movement of securities begins after normal business hours by the DTCC, a company affiliated to the NSCC.

After normal business hours on $T+2$ the NSCC provides the DTCC with a report of the securities that must be transferred by NSCC members. During the transfer process, all securities will move through the NSCC's holding account at the DTCC (e.g., from member A to the DTCC then on to member B). The NSCC acts as a counterparty and will guarantee all securities transfers.

On $T+3$ (third business day after expiry), the NSCC nets all financial obligations of each member so that only one payment or receipt is needed from each member. The NSCC again stands in the middle of all payments/ receipts. By the end of $T+3$, all payments and deliveries will have been completed.

OneChicago

This brand new exchange, made up of the combined forces of Chicago's finest exchanges, to all intents and purposes uses the same delivery process as the NQLX, but differs in that the OCC does the clearing then hands the process on to the NSCC and the DTCC.

OneChicago trades by means of CBOEdirect and GLOBEX front ends.

CBOEdirect is the front end part of OneChicago's technological need to provide a powerful match engine that is designed to work with their Lead Market Maker system and cope with what they hope will be large volumes and a steadily increasing product base. CBOEdirect was first developed for the CBOE options market in 2002 and is a slightly newer system than LIFFE's Connect™, which was first deployed in 1999. Nevertheless, both systems have considerable processing power and can be rightly regarded as absolutely top-class systems in current financial markets. GLOBEX is the joint venture between the Chicago Mercantile Exchange and Reuters and is the front end screen-based sytem through which CME members have traded electronically for several years.

Euronext LIFFE

Euronext LIFFE's futures contracts are cash-settled, and all clearing and the cash settlement process is undertaken by the LCH. The cash settlement model makes the whole process fairly simple, given the wide-ranging array of European and US stocks in Euronext LIFFE's portfolio. The only exceptions are the Scandinavian contracts that were changed to physical delivery in November 2002.

MEFF

MEFF has always been a screen-based market since its establishment in November 1989 with all settlements (both cash and physical) highly automated. The exchange, like Euronext LIFFE, has had many years of experience in physical options settlement.

It has its own electronic system, which is also used by the Portuguese market. MEFF is different in that the client can elect to have cash or physical delivery. Whether he or she gets it, is another matter, as can be seen below!

MEFF acts as its own clearing house. Spain adopted a single company model in the legal form of a holding company that integrates all the processes necessary to organizing trading, settlement, and clearing.

Definition of the preference of the account holder

SSFs contracts are settled at expiration by delivery of shares or by cash differences. Holders must communicate in advance of expiration their preferences for physical or cash settlement. Holders with open accounts in the MEFF system are presumed to prefer the delivery method, unless they expressly communicate their preference for cash settlement. New-account holders have to communicate their preference for one of the alternatives when they open a new account. In any case, this preference can be changed from one expiration to another and is applicable to all futures registered in the holder's account.

Both sides of a contract must be settled by the same method, therefore a cash settlement will apply to the highest possible number of open positions of those holders who preferred that method. However (and here's the rub for cash-settlers!), the excess will be settled by delivery. Naturally, all positions pertaining to holders who preferred the delivery method are also settled through delivery.

Therefore, determination of whether contracts should be settled by cash or by delivery depends on the number of contracts that were settled by differences in the lowest figures of:

● long contracts whose holders have chosen cash settlement; or
● short contracts whose holders have chosen cash settlement.

In order to determine the counterparties of the contracts to be cash settled, a random method of assignment is employed. For that purpose, all the positions of all holders preferring cash settlement will be put in order, grouped by holder. In the event that the number of contracts on each side (long and short) are the same, then no random ballot is required. If the number is not the same, there is a draw to decide which counterparty side has an imbalance of more contracts, until there is a direct balance between the sides desiring cash settlement. The residue of contracts seeking cash settlement that cannot be so settled will be left to assignment and physical delivery.

Naturally, therefore, the number of contracts that are settled by delivery is the sum of the number of contracts mentioned above as well as the contracts whose holders have opted for settlement by delivery. In other words, at all times there is essentially an in-built preference toward physical delivery in the MEFF contracts, of which only those seeking cash settlement ought to be aware.

For those contracts that do achieve cash settlement, this is made in cash for the difference with respect to the reference price, which will be the same as the settlement price of the contract on expiry.

For deliverable contracts, settlement is as follows: SSFs contracts are settled at expiration by delivery of the underlying shares for each class of contract. The shares to be delivered are only those admitted to the list that have full rights fungible with the principal share series of the stock (naturally a common issue for all physical deliverables!).

Delivery of shares takes place only at one price, namely the reference price. The combination of the daily settlement of profits and losses (variation margin) with the delivery at the reference price results in a purchase or sale at precisely the futures price traded on the original transaction (together with any adjustments made for corporate actions).

At expiration, any necessary stock transactions will be done by MEFF to assign the stock transaction, while endeavouring:

• to minimize the volume of transactions;
• to offset buy-and-sell obligations within the same account;
• to match opposing transactions between different accounts of the same member.

Once the delivery transaction has taken place, the position ceases to be a futures contact and becomes a cash stock market transaction with all the consequences, according to the relevant rules and procedures. MEFF will then notify the Sociedad de Bolsas, in its capacity as the company running the Stock Exchange Interconnection System, of the trades in the underlying security that as a consequence of the expiration of futures must take place.

The reference price (delivery price)

On settlement at expiration of the contracts, MEFF gives instructions to the members on the share trades to be effected. These trades must take place at the reference price.

The reference price is the closing price of the corresponding stock at the Stock Exchange Interconnection System on the expiration date as published by the Sociedad de Bolsas.

India

The National Stock Exchange (NSE) is a cash-settled market and therefore very similar in operations to Euronext LIFFE. It began trading a basket of some 29 stocks at the time of writing on November 9th, 2001. For expiry purposes, the final settlement price is the closing price of the underlying security in its last half hour of trading on expiry day, on a VWAP basis. As ever beware of the contract size; remember, they are all different.

South Africa

With around 60 SSFs listed and having begun trading in 1999, South Africa has been a hotbed of equity derivatives innovations with various structured products proving popular with investors on the Johannesburg Stock Exchange (JSE). Interestingly, the South African Exchange (formerly the independent SAFEX, but now a division of the JSE) also lists American-style options on

SSFs. American options permit the holders to exercise their options at any time before and including expiry while European options are less flexible and permit exercise into the underlying only at expiry.

Physical settlement is the order of the day in South Africa with margins at around 10%. Trading takes place through the automated trading system—an auction-based system, matched automatically on the basis of price and time. Expiry is the third Thursday of the contract month. The expiration valuation method is the average price as calculated by the JSE between 14:00 hours and 16:00 hours on the expiration date.

Singapore

Cash settlement is employed in Singapore and margins are around 20%, like the American markets. The Singapore Exchange incorporates its own clearing house.

Portugal

The BVLP uses the same trading system as MEFF in Spain and lists seven stock futures with exclusively physical settlement and a three-day delivery cycle. Last trading day is the third Friday of the contract month. The settlement price is a weighted average calculated by the number of contracts of the last 12 deals by their traded prices. SSFs began in Portugal in 1997 with Telefonica Portugal and the local electricity utility EDP. Interestingly, a stock repo market was introduced in April 1997, and then in September 1998 the BVLP introduced securities-lending, thus allowing the exchange to offer members OTC and exchange-traded strategies on the same exchange for futures and options. An interesting footnote is that equity options were actually introduced after the launch of SSFs at BVLP, in this case in September 1999.

Greece

The Athens ADX uses a trading system called OASIS, which is based on Sweden's OM system. Margin requirements vary between 15% and 20 + % and is calculated using a SPAN-style system called RIVA (not to be mistaken for the fine Italian wooden launches beloved of yacht owners on the French and Italian Riviera!). Expiry is the third Friday of the contract month, and there is a three-day delivery cycle handled via the Athens Exchange's own clearing house. Note that, somewhat like Portugal, the ADX also has an efficient repo and reverse repo market in equities that was introduced to help compensate for what are regarded locally as idiosyncrasies in the cash market.

Australia

The Sydney Futures Exchange (SFE) has products called Individual Share Futures (ISFs), which are cleared through the SFE's own clearing house. With the rival Australian Stock Exchange merging its clearing operations into one organization, the possibility remains that ASX may choose to list SSFs and trump the SFE, given its superior position with existing cash market players.

Russia

The relative immaturity of Russian capital markets probably does not seem like a very likely location for the trading of SSFs, but in fact various local factors have helped generate considerable interest in SSFs there. Both MICEX (Moscow Interbank Currency Exchange) and RTS (Russian Trading System) have listed SSFs, with RTS being more successful to date. Leading Russian stocks such as energy company Lukoil have proven popular as SSFs among Russian speculative traders who find the simple settlement procedures of margined futures easy to transact compared with buying and settling cash equities. It is an interesting issue that while overall we would expect SSFs to be a product of highly mature markets, even in rapidly developing ones such as Russia, they can play a key role in risk transfer and aiding liquidity.

CLOSING PRICES

Perhaps the best method of price discovery is the closing auction—where essentially a separate session takes place during a predetermined closing period—which can be 10, 20, or more minutes at the end of the session. Each auction process can be slightly different, so it pays to check every one. Alas, it is beyond the scope of this book to examine every exchange's opening or closing auction process in details. However, there can be some differences in terms of weighting, of which price becomes the settlement figure.

In the case of Euronext LIFFE, which offers the broadest portfolio of SSFs under its USFs banner, the settlement prices are agreed as shown in Table 6.1.

VWAP is a term that appears frequently in Table 6.1 and often leads to some confusion. VWAP is a process that is frequently instituted by the derivatives exchange to achieve a fair value for settlement relating to a price where considerable volume is traded—as opposed merely to an extreme price in late trading where very little may have actually traded. VWAP is calculated by adding the value of the shares traded within a given time and then dividing

Table 6.1   Exchange Delivery Settlement Price (EDSP).

Denmark	VWAP of trades during the last 10 minutes of trading on Copenhagen exchanges
Finland	VWAP of trades during the last 10 minutes of trading on Helsinki exchanges
France	Official closing auction price on Euronext Paris
Germany	Official closing auction price on Deutsche Börse
Ireland	Closing Auction Price on the Irish Stock Exchange
Italy	Opening auction price on Borsa Italiana on third Friday of the delivery month
Netherlands	Official closing price on Euronext Amsterdam
Norway	VWAP of trades during the last 10 minutes of trading on Oslo exchanges
Spain	Official closing price on Bolsa de Madrid
Sweden	Official closing price on Stockholmsborsen
Switzerland	Official closing price on Virt-X
US	USFs: VWAP of trades from NYSE and NASDAQ during first 10 minutes of trading on last trading day

by the number of shares traded. Obviously, where **VWAP** is higher, is where the exchange will seek to settle its market, because it suggests a greater level of market activity. The measure is also popular with pension funds for analysing where there is depth of liquidity in the stock market.

7
Single Stock Futures and Indices

If anything has truly shaped investor activity in the past 20 years, it has been the massive surge in indices. Nowadays, the Dow Jones average does not merely reflect the health of Wall Street, it is in fact an interchangeable term for the stock market itself. In the modern investment environment, stock indices have developed enormously to become a core facet of contemporary markets. Indeed, in the past decade, the process of indexation has become a veritable mania in every aspect of financial markets.

Stock indices fall into two core areas: broad- and narrow-based indices. Broad-based indices have traditionally tended to reflect the largest stocks on a major national marketplace, such as the Dow Jones average and S&P 500 in the USA (admittedly the latter broader than the former!) or the FTSE 100 in the UK (pedants will delight in noting that the FT-All Share was actually the first UK index, but its calculation method made it difficult to adapt, especially for the real-time environment of derivatives.

In the early days of index-trading, there were all sorts of rough-and-ready guides to approximate one index for another—one could garner a rough Dow Jones indication by multiplying the daily move in the S&P 500 by a factor between 7 and 8, for instance. That was back in the days when the most sophisticated mathematical processing power on a trader's desk was likely to be his HP 12 C calculator. Nowadays, in increasingly digital markets, software abounds to produce precise index calculations in real time. Nevertheless, thanks to historical legacy, some very old indices remain popular (with the Dow Jones Industrial Average the granddaddy of them all, having been first formulated by the pioneering *Wall Street Journal* editor Charles Dow in the late 19th century). While nowadays index calculation is fairly similar in the modern indices, it is worth having a quick look at some key indices in which there are components with Single Stock Futures (SSFs) listed.

DOW JONES 30 INDUSTRIAL AVERAGE

Commonly known as the "Dow", the "DJ", or the "DJIA", the Dow Jones 30 industrial average is based on 30 US blue-chip companies. To the pedantic it is not strictly speaking an index, because there is no base year for its value to be set at an arbitrary number, such as 100. Rather, the Dow Jones is an arithmetical price-weighted average, in which component weightings are affected only by changes in the stocks' prices, in stark contrast to other indices that are affected by both price changes and changes in the number of outstanding shares. It started in 1884 with 11 shares and expanded to a dozen in June 1886. In October 1928, it further expanded to 30 shares and has remained this size ever since (although the actual component companies themselves have changed quite considerably!). The components are selected at the discretion of the editors of the *Wall Street Journal*, and there are no predetermined criteria except that the components should be established US companies that are leaders in their industries. Note that while the Dow Jones Industrial Average tends to hog the limelight there are two other Dow Jones averages—the Transport and Utilities indices—which while less commonly observed nowadays (when invented Transport and Utilities were go-go sectors akin to the dotcoms and telcos in more recent times) are nevertheless popular among analysts of Dow Theory—a sort of technical analysis approach using the various Dow indices.

S&P 500 COMPOSITE INDEX

Introduced in 1957, the S&P 500 is calculated using a base-weighted aggregate methodology, which means the level of the index reflects the total market value of all 500 component stocks relative to a particular base period. The total market value of a company is determined by multiplying the price of the stock by the number of outstanding shares. An index of a set of combined variables, such as price and numbers of shares, is labelled a composite index by statisticians. Promotion to and regulation from the index is done on a constant basis.

NASDAQ COMPOSITE INDEX

The NASDAQ Composite first appeared on February 5th, 1971 and tracks all the shares traded on the NASDAQ. It is a capitalization-weighted index, so the index's value is based on the total market value of all the issues that compose the index. The NASDAQ Composite is also a ratio, based on the relationship between the total market value of all the stocks that compose the index today and the total value on the first day the index was issued. To calculate the value of the index, the current market value (the sum of the price times the total shares outstanding for each security) is divided by the market value on day 1 of the index. Admittance to and deletions from the list are done on an ongoing basis.

FTSE 100 INDEX

The "Footsie" was inaugurated on December 31st, 1983 with a base of 1,000. As the name implies it contains the 100 largest market capitalized stocks on the London Stock Exchange. It is an arithmetical-weighted index where the weights are market capitalization. Interestingly, the index is computed using the average of the best bid and best offer quotes rather than the last traded price method. Therefore, the index can actually rise or fall without any trading, which is slightly bizarre! The components are revised every quarter with relegation and promotion decided by a panel. Promotion and relegation is not automatic, but is generally assured around a bracket of the bottom four in the index and the top four just outside it.

DEUTSCHE AKTIENINDEX DAX

The DAX is an index of the 30 largest German companies quoted on the Frankfurt Stock Exchange and was introduced in 1988. It is a "total return" index in that it measures the returns from dividends as well as share price performance. It is a capitalization-weighted total return index calculated using the Laspeyres index method.

INTERNATIONAL INDICES

Nowadays, some of the stock indices are broader than mere national boundaries. After unsuccesssful beginnings with pan-European stock indices in the late 1980s and early 1990s (e.g., the FTSE Eurotrack), various providers have been battling for dominance of the European index sector. With the advent of the euro (which encompasses most but not all leading European stocks— British shares, for instance, remain sterling-denominated), the vogue for pan-European stock-investing has created the first truly cross-border regional marketplace—even if it remains in its infancy at the time of writing.

DOW JONES EUROSTOXX 50

The Dow Jones EUROTOXX index was introduced in February 1998 and has been by far the most successful of the cross-border indices. There are 50 stocks, which cover all components of the 18 Dow Jones EUROSTOXX market sector indices. The Dow Jones EUROSTOXX market sector indices represent the eurozone portion of the Dow Jones STOXX Total Market Index, which in turn covers over 95% of the total market capitalization of the stocks traded on the major exchanges of 17 European countries. The index is weighted by free-float market capitalization. Each component's weight is capped at 10% of the index's total free-float market capitalization. The weightings are reviewed quarterly, while the composition of the index is reviewed annually in September.

MSCI INDICES

The Morgan Stanley Capital International (MSCI) indices are becoming more and more widely recognized and they are the preferred benchmark of many major fund managers around the world. This is in part due to the collaboration between MSCI and S&P to produce the Global Industry Classification Standard. Funds are very focused nowadays on measurements made against standard recognized benchmarks. MSCI calculates many indices, but generally speaking they are free-float adjusted and market capitalization calculated. The indices are reviewed quarterly and often have a significant effect on the markets, as shares are brought in or drop out of the index.

PROMOTION AND RELEGATION

As can be noted from all the above indices, they are consistently updated to reflect the changing fortunes of different companies. Traders will do well to keep abreast of the likely changes to any index if only because there will be more listed SSFs that fall outside these indices as SSFs develop or, indeed, listed SSFs that will fall out of the index. The latter is important because, while a stock may lose considerable value before falling out of an index, once its departure from an index is confirmed it can often result in the market falling further as index-tracking fund managers seek to replace it with the new share. Similarly, the new share will often experience a bullish run as it approaches entry to the index (especially once confirmed), as fund managers seek to buy that share. Of course, recalling our discussion of interpolated hedging in Chapter 3 on trading, readers will immediately see that SSFs can be very beneficial for index-tracking fund managers who try to alter their portfolio ahead of index changes. They may seek, for instance, to sell SSFs ahead of the changes and then deliver the shares, perhaps because they wish to take a dividend just ahead of the index change or simply because they find it easier to have an alternative method to ease their holding of the stock. Likewise, buying SSFs ahead of a stock being added to an index can be a very simple way to ensure a fund has the upside covered, while effectively using margin to manage their cash position so the index changes do not overly impact their returns. All indices are constantly changing, and, in the event of a merger between two companies in one major index, it is important to remember that a substitution may take place very rapidly. The key issue for traders to be wary of is not to be caught in the volatility backlash when shares move in or out of an index as they will tend to fall when leaving an index, and rise when entering one, regardless of the fundamentals of their trading position or even of the broad stock market.

FREE FLOAT

A major issue for stock indices around the world in recent years has been that of "free float"—in other words, how many shares of a particular company are actually likely to be traded and how many are closely held and therefore unlikely to be traded on the open market. Many indices underwent significant change, particularly during 2000/2001, as those stocks that had very small free floats were reweighted and even relegated from indices entirely; they were not felt to be sufficiently tradable compared with shares in slightly smaller, but more disparately held corporations.

NARROW-BASED INDICES

While the vogue for large-scale indices that can be tracked to assess macro-trends has reached a modicum of maturity (even though prospects continue to look encouraging for continued growth), the major area of recent development has been in the business of narrow-based indices. Such narrow-based indices generally tend to reflect a single stock market sector (e.g., pharmaceuticals or automobiles).

The introduction of narrow-based index futures at the same time as the introduction of SSFs in the USA should be a boost to fund managers who, in their selection process, often focus on their key preferred sector before deciding on a particular stock. Narrow-based indices allow managers to at least gain a snapshot of the relative health of the components in a sector before they invest. There are also a series of narrow-based index derivatives on EUREX, although that exchange as you recall has long been somewhat agnostic about SSFs. For instance, on OneChicago there are 15 sector futures:

- aerospace;
- banks;
- biotechnology;
- communications technology;
- diversified financial;
- electric utilities;
- diversified industrial;
- investment services;
- mining and metals;
- oil companies;
- pharmaceuticals;
- retail;
- semiconductors;
- software;
- technology hardware and equipment.

Each index is physically settled against the basket of shares in the sector, and each sector is represented by between three and nine stocks from that sector. Margin is set at 20% of the basket value. Naturally, opportunities abound for fund managers to employ cash stock or, more simply, SSFs to modify their anticipated returns from an index by either substituting or subtracting stocks from the existing narrow-based index family.

NARROW-BASED INDEX CONSTRUCTION

Narrow-based indices are constructed by selecting a series of stocks from a particular economic sector to become deliverable components of the index. In the case of the OneChicago exchange, for instance, it follows an approximately equal dollar-weighted approach when constructing narrow-based indices.

Using the dollar-weighted approach, the quantity of shares of the deliverable components of the index is weighted to approximately equalize the cash value contribution of each index constituent (Table 7.1). OneChicago uses simple, linear, dollar weightings, with the results rounded to the nearest 100 shares. Therefore, a stock trading at $15 per share would have approximately twice as many shares in a OneChicago narrow-based index as a stock trading at $30 per share.

In Table 7.2, Stock 3 is trading at a price that is approximately 11.4 times higher than the price of Stock 5. In order to create an approximately equal

Table 7.1   Index values and prices.

The cash value of each index component is the cash market price of a single share of the component's underlying security multiplied by the number of deliverable shares of that security in the index.
The cash value of the index itself is the sum of all index component values.
The devisor (or multiplier) for all OneChicago narrow-based indices is 500. The theoretical cash price of the index is therefore determined by dividing the cash value of the index by 500.
The minimum price change (tick size) is $0.01. The results in a tick value of $5.00 ($0.01 × 500 = $5.00).

Table 7.2   Example index.

Index component	Cash price ($)	Shares in index	Value ($)
Stock 1	24.32	300	7,296
Stock 2	27.40	300	8,220
Stock 3	84.00	100	8,400
Stock 4	16.75	500	8,375
Stock 5	7.34	1,100	8,074
Cash value of index			40,365
Divisor		500	
Cash price of index	80.73		

dollar-weighted index, there are therefore 11 times as many shares of Stock 5 as Stock 3 (11 × 100 = 1,100 when rounded off to the nearest 100 shares).

When the cash values of all the components of the index are added together, the sum is $40,365. Dividing this by 500 (the divisor) results in a theoretical cash price of $80.73 for the index.

EXPIRY EFFECTS AND TRIPLE-WITCHING

As stock indices and SSFs are all inherently interrelated, one interesting effect from the different markets will be how they expire when the SSF and narrow-based index markets reach a degree of maturity. SSFs expire on the third Friday of the last trading month of a contract at the same time as various narrow indices, broad indices, and individual equity options. When the equity options, index options, and index futures all expire at the same time, this is known as "triple-witching". There have been instances in the past of markets being quite volatile when they reach the expiry point and of squeezes in particular issues distorting prices in the run-up to expiry. Watching the open interest in particular markets is a good precaution to take here in an attempt to ensure that squeezes do not happen. Indeed, in an effort to try and reduce the possibilities of squeezes, the US SSFs exchanges have instituted position limits for the last five days of the contract's trading. In the case of OneChicago, for instance, this is either 13,500 net contracts or 22,500 net contracts (long or short), as per Commodities Futures Trading Commission requirements, during the last five days of trading in that market. Incidentally, cash settlement makes the possibility of a squeeze greater, as of course borrowing stock for delivery may be difficult in certain markets.

INDEX REPLICATION

When it comes to trading stock indices, derivatives players have found it very beneficial to play the relationship between the cash and futures prices by replicating indices with cash. However, the addition of SSFs to a trader's armoury provides a whole new range of opportunities for the trader, as suddenly a new instrument can be used to replicate indices and do so on a much more cash-efficient basis, thanks to margin, than merely buying stocks. Of course, with larger indices, the issue is not to buy or sell the entire index, as this would be far too costly and difficult to achieve in a few moments. Rather, the aim is to replicate indices in a slightly "quick and dirty" fashion to achieve essentially the same overall return as an index produces, but by cherry-picking only those key, vitally important stocks that more or less precisely replicate the index's behaviour. This process revolves around what is known as "beta". The second letter of the Greek alphabet, beta, measures the relative performance of a stock within an index (as already mentioned, the first letter, alpha, reflects absolute performance). Therefore a stock may be less sensitive than an index over time, while another can be more sensitive to moves in the index. Overall, the total beta of all the stocks must add up to 1, as the whole index reflects what all its components do to a measure of unity.

In particular, on US exchanges with narrow indices, where only three to nine stocks make up each index on average, the possibility of replicating those indices is fairly simple, in some cases even using all the components. However, with the likes of the FTSE 100 or the S&P 500, a proxy package of shares is absolutely necessary! When executing programme trades for index arbitrage, obviously the fewer shares required to replicate the index the better as the execution risk is reduced.

When it comes to SSFs, exchanges have naturally had their minds focused on index replication from the very start, and, to this end, new additions to the US markets in particular, from the inception of NQLX and OneChicago, have been heavily oriented toward covering as many different narrow indices as possible. At Euronext LIFFE, where the world's only truly international portfolio of SSFs exists, uppermost in their thought process has been the concept of ensuring broader exposure to the leading EUROSTOXX indices. Trying to match this demand from equity and hedge funds, LIFFE has managed a quite remarkable range of coverage for their 115 offerings to date across various indices.

At the time of writing, the Euronext LIFFE portfolio of Universal Stock Futures (USFs) covered 13 countries and had a combined market capitalization exceeding $7.93 trillion. The stocks account for 94% of the EUROTOXX 50 index and 67.26% of the FTSE 100 index. Naturally, these 115 different international stocks easily lend themselves to permitting index arbitrage and other similar replication strategies. As Euronext LIFFE has the broadest portfolio of stocks, it seemed best to focus on their exchange with a view to perusing a few leading indices and seeing how they can be effectively replicated using existing SSFs.

Indeed, with the opening of SSFs in the USA in late November 2002, it will be interesting to see just how many new, narrow-based indices are listed both in Europe and the USA in the short term—we expect there to be a plethora. It will be simple to replicate many of these predominantly sector indices with SSFs. Overall, the process of correlating narrow-based indices with perhaps fewer than a dozen contracts will be simple for readers to understand as long as they grasp the concepts outlined below for indices that are somewhat more macro. In the remainder of this section we will examine two major indices: the pan-European titans of the emerging pan-European index market, the Eurotop 100, and the Dow Jones EUROSTOXX 50.

In the case of the EUROSTOXX 50 index, it is already almost entirely covered by LIFFE's USFs. Apart from Endesa, St Gobain, and Repsol, all the other 47 components of the index can be readily traded via LIFFE USFs. Given that St Gobain has long been a very healthily traded option on the former MONEP division of what is now Euronext Paris, this may yet be given an SSF in the near future. Anyway, just looking at the current state of LIFFE's USFs, if we took the whole 47 stocks and used them as a basket, the end result would be a remarkably proximate beta value. However—and please don't do this without prior reference to a proper index arbitrageur—using a handful or more of the existing LIFFE USFs can provide a pretty good proxy for the index. However, once again please seek supervision and don't rely on our word before going out and building your own index proxies.

By way of a very hasty example, a clutch of stocks like Carrefour, DaimlerChrysler, ING, Munich Re, Sanofi, and Vivendi gets us very close to a replication of sorts with only six stocks. The sum of the six betas incidentally is: 0.905, 1.1, 1.304, 0.876, 0.673, 1.146 = 6.004 (divide them by 6 and you get slightly over 1, indicating remarkable proximity to the index's actual movement).

Of course, we haven't really made much allowance here for relative liquidity, and doubtless many index replicators would be more likely, for instance, to choose an Italian stock that has traditionally been a bit more liquid among LIFFE's USFs than some other contracts. When it comes to index arbitrage and so forth, it is not merely sufficient to have the betas correct, one also needs to choose a stock that is regularly at the most highly liquid end of the market-place (to ensure swift, cheap security of dealing). Thus, one liquid stock's beta may be much more valuable than a less liquid or difficult-to-borrow stock for short-sellers. Of course, in the world of SSFs the issue of borrowing to sell short is removed, thus helping index "replicators" to find a broader choice of potential shorts when trying to sell the components and buy the index.

We would like to point out that we are just trying to make an illustration here, before readers get on their high horse and start to complain that we just don't understand enough about index replication to be let loose on the subject.

Meanwhile, on the Eurotop 100, no fewer than 79 of the current Eurotop stocks are listed as USFs. Of the omissions, a couple actually have LIFFE options listed on them, but not yet USFs. In many respects the difficulty with index replication is that product development and introduction needs to go through a complete market cycle to ensure comprehensiveness. For instance, with SSFs really only being introduced on a serious basis in the late dotcom/ telecom mania of 2000, there is a relative paucity of less volatile, more established "old economy" (as opposed to "new economy") stocks, such as mining, resource, and heavy industrial companies. Also, if you want to ensure slightly greater index comprehensiveness, you can find two of the Eurotop components that are not listed on Euronext LIFFE (Endesa and Repsol) listed in the Spanish MEFF exchange's USFs portfolio. In time, as an economic/market cycle completes, expect the SSFs listings to more accurately reflect all the components of a broad index.

There are a couple of other unique issues. For instance, Eurotop lists a couple of shares where two classes are included in the index: for instance, both Fortis A and B shares are included. LIFFE USFs are available on the Fortis A shares, while the B shares are a unique domestic class listed only on Euronext Belgium. Similarly, Roche splits into a local share (RO) listed as SwX and ROG (which is the international variant that has a USF based on it and trades on the London-based Virt-X exchange).

Once again, it is not difficult to spot a fairly vast array of possible packages of shares/USFs that can be utilized to replicate the index. Given the cheap, efficient, and simple qualities of exploiting USFs in long or short equity strategies, we know of many intelligent folk who are already happily replicating indices such as the Eurotop 100 and EUROSTOXX 50. In order to give you a chance to at least paper-trade some evaluation of how you can exploit such trades using Eurotop and USFs.

As indices are created from individual equities, there is of course a very close fundamental relationship between cash stocks and indices. SSFs add an extra dimension to this entire relationship, and for budding index arbitrageurs, or traders seeking to modify returns from an index, the cash-efficient possibilities as a result of using SSFs are indeed simply enormous.

Conclusion

THE NEXT STEPS, THE ULTIMATE PROSPECTS FOR SINGLE STOCK FUTURES

The Single Stock Futures (SSFs) revolution is in its infancy. Quite whether it will ever achieve its potential remains to be seen. In Europe, the development of the product was accompanied by significant marketing initiatives, which at least cemented a broad-based understanding of the product. In the USA, the product launched at the end of 2002 in a way that could best be described as distinctly muted. Of course, it may have been that concerns over whether the first broad-based electronic US futures exchanges would actually work as they were supposed to may have been a key concern and whether NQLX and OneChicago will yet up their marketing programmes to actually reach out to the wider world rather than merely seeking to sell to the tiny world of existing futures investors.

At the Swiss Futures and Options Exchange (SFOE) annual meeting in Burgenstock in 2002, the CEO of EUREX (a noted sceptic on the benefits of SSFs it ought to be noted), Rudi Ferscha was quite correct when he stated that: "Derivatives are expanding into the firmament of financial markets."

Nevertheless, the fact remains that the futures markets are perceived in a bad light by the vast majority of American investors and indeed a great bulk of US financial professionals. The reason that CBOT has its slots on CNBC is probably more to do with the fact that the fading open outcry pits provide a veritable televisual feast, while simple streaming numbers on plasma screens at NASDAQ do not.

SSFs are products that can help bridge the gulf that exists between the great many traditional cash market investors, both professional and retail. In the past (and not without justification – albeit truly a generation or more ago), futures markets were regarded as somewhat of a casino (with an insider mass who are there to control prices), which a minority of misguided outsiders are suckered into losing money in. A harsh viewpoint? Indeed, this is an absolutely inaccurate one and the Commodities Futures Trading Commission and NFA[1] as well as the exchanges in the USA have done much to ensure that in many ways regulation of brokers and dealers is at least as well if not arguably better policed than in the cash securities industry. Nevertheless, public perception is fickle and until there is a widespread campaign to change that attitude, it will continue to fester in the public imagination. The launch of SSFs provides the single best opportunity to do so. Yet, it was clearly evident within a few days of launching SSFs that the US financial markets were largely shrouded in ignorance about their launch.[2]

Aside from all that juicy speculation out there in financial markets, the issue of risk transfer has of course long been a focal point of the derivatives business. Of late, various innovations (such as Basle 2 and a host of national regulatory measures) have gradually been trying to push trading off Over The Counter (OTC) and onto exchanges. The EU Undertakings for Collective Investment in Transferable Securities (UCITS) guidelines have been continually beefed up with a view to controlling risk on OTC instruments by pension fund, unit trust, and mutual fund investors. Given that the issue of meeting pensions obligations for investors remains pivotal for the governments of all the world's major economies, the issue of ensuring probity in investment will similarly become increasingly important during this decade.

Of course, the whole question of just what is a fair balance in risk management terms for OTC products remains one of the most emotionally charged issues in financial markets. Banks want to retain an adults-only marketplace for their own dealings, and indeed it is difficult to argue that consenting adult institutions ought to be allowed to do their own thing in private ... although given that adult club members have included the likes of Barings Bank, BCCI, and so forth, one is inclined to be a tad concerned about counterparty risk even if only as a retail banking customer! Then again, as the sage folk would note, while the likes of collapsed hedge fund LTCM threatened to rip a hole in the world's banking balance sheets when it collapsed, the (admittedly less expensive) demise of Barings through on-exchange transactions made barely a ripple by comparison in financial markets, thanks to Nick Leeson's foibles being entirely on-exchange and therefore Central Counterparty Processing (CCP) cleared.

Perhaps one of the more interesting issues is how the measures seek to

---

[1] National Futures Association, the organization that regulates traders in US commodity/futures markets.
[2] We thank Neal Weintraub and Perry Dahm for bringing our attention to the fact that the nationally syndicated US radio financial show *Moneytalk with Bob Brinker* broadcast that SSFs "were experimental and had not started trading yet" in late November, some days after their launch.

restrict counterparty risk on portfolios so that only 5% to 10% of assets in any person's pension scheme are held with one counterparty. Similarly, the guidelines are concerned with the spread of risk that would affect anybody holding, for instance, the bonds, warrants, and cash equity of a particular single company. However, it is perhaps the counterparty risk issue that could become the most significant for OTC equity derivatives markets, and this is ultimately likely to benefit the SSFs environment. The issue with Contracts For Difference (CFDs), for instance, is a key one, as pension fund managers may need to split their holdings across multiple managers whereas they can deal more flexibly via the exchange and clearing house for SSFs. Naturally, the sheer logistics alone of holding multiple CFD positions with different brokers may prove to be an irritant to the pension funds, presumably leading to greater exchange trade. In particular, whereas SSF positions can in fact be executed through any broker on an exchange such as LIFFE, CFDs need to be executed through the broker with whom they were first opened.

True, the overall impact of the UCITS guidelines won't affect the ordinary account holders in CFDs, but overall such moves will push liquidity toward the exchanges if institutions find it more economical to deal through these markets.

The economic advantages for trading in the leading SSFs will doubtless start to win over business from the OTC providers. Nevertheless, the flexibility of CFDs in providing access to a wider range of stocks not already listed on exchanges will remain.

Another issue in the overall risk transfer issue is of course inextricably linked with CCP. However, regulators are now beginning to tighten up, and in this respect it is pension fund managers and trustees who can find themselves at risk if they make an oversight. For instance, the movement for trustees to be responsible for scrutinizing every counterparty in a pension fund portfolio is gaining pace especially within Europe. In this respect, the merits of CCP have suddenly become a great deal more transparent to many trustees who don't wish to run the risk of seeing a supposedly solid counterparty biodegrade. In this respect, once again the advantage appears to lie solidly with SSFs products as opposed to their OTC cousins.

Overall, as more regulations are likely to encourage the use of exchanges for various reasons, it would seem safe to presume that this will be to the advantage of all investors seeking sound risk transfer, hedging, and speculative opportunities in equity markets through SSFs.

SSFs can and will grow generically, but they require a massive education effort even within professional markets. To date the will has simply not been demonstrated within the US exchanges to go out and sell the product—yet SSFs probably need just as hard a sales effort as the original financial futures markets ... only in this case the marketplace is a much, much vaster one and indeed the many vested interests keen to see SSFs disappear must have been relieved that the initial marketing effort for SSFs has been so weak in the world's largest marketplace.

Put simply, the initiative that is SSFs needs to be nurtured and either the exchanges can go for a softly softly, approach over several years waiting for volume to build (and hope their increasingly return-driven, profit-seeking shareholders are willing to maintain their backing) or they can become more proactively involved with the broad marketplace in selling their product.

True, one thing that has largely remained constant throughout the three-decade development of on-exchange financial and equity derivatives has been the fact that the time to reach a degree of mature liquidity in a market remains the same. In the old days it may have taken 18 months to 2 years to reach all the prerequisite players and convince them of the merits of the product. Nowadays, exchanges are much better able (although still not as comprehensively as some might think) to discern just who their end-users are and reach out to them in marketing campaigns. However, now that risk management is much more holistic and driven by the vast trading arms of financial institutions, it is clear that even where an institution may truly desire to trade an instrument at the earliest possible date, many will be precluded by the need to meet certain defined liquidity issues (usually these will vary from institution, to institution but the market basically must be demonstrating an ability to trade a size appropriate to the needs of the institution concerned). Once these liquidity thresholds are met, the traders are still required to refer their demand for new trading limits to centralized risk committees, which often only meet monthly and even then tend to ensure they have employed very adequate due diligence before they grant any new trading limits. Integrated risk management and processing software can also mean delays to granting limits. Overall, the net process means that it is still generally about 18 months to 2 years before many major players can enter established markets. In this case, the really exciting growth phase of SSFs will likely not take place until mid-2004 at the earliest.

Having said that, those traders who can get into a marketplace as close to the ground floor as possible and perceive the changes to a market as it develops are in absolutely the best position to learn, adapt, and ultimately profit from that environment. If you can access SSFs markets, it makes sense to enter them now, because each day of experience helps give you an edge over institutions that arrive later.

Product launch was the one area in which the US market made rapid progress. With a potential pool of hundreds of US equities alone, the launch day saw only 30 different individual equities listed on NQLX and 21 on OneChicago, but within days both NQLX and OneChicago were aggressively adding new stocks to their lists. However, of course the key to developing SSFs remains balancing the twin needs of broad product-offering against a sound modicum of liquidity. And that brings us right back to the key question of just how cohesively the US exchanges can educate their investing community, both retail and professional. The future of SSFs in many ways is dependent on the strength of their development in the USA, as huge liquidity there will ultimately drive the products elsewhere in the world.

Indeed, with US margins vastly higher than those in Europe, the ironic possibility remains that the US market may yet suffer a loss of volume to overseas markets if investors seek to minimize their margin exposures. The prospect of intense competition for US liquidity may yet emerge if the US marketplace continues to price margins not on a risk-adjusted basis, but on what the competing regulators feel sits comfortably with their core constituencies—in the case of higher SSFs margins, the stock-lenders and cash equity brokers who want to try and throttle the product at birth.

Margin arbitrage, like regulatory arbitrage, may yet become a big issue in the next phase of SSFs development. Will there be a second stage? Well, we believe so, despite the relatively poor initial marketing of the product in the USA. The issue for the marketplace remains the simple one that was crystallized by Sir Brian Williamson when he pioneered LIFFE's international Universal Stock Futures products in 2000. The revolution was all about the issues of a product that was "simple, cheap, and efficient". SSFs retain precisely these key advantages, and, provided they are properly promoted and not subject to renewed regulatory strangulation, they can become a pillar of the financial markets, adding to liquidity and enhancing the depth of equity markets, providing huge profit opportunities for speculators, offering a multiplicity of strategies for investors of all shapes and sizes, while being a product that helps make cash equity-dealing better for every investor.

> *SSFs have been portrayed in this report as a new stage in the evolution of financial derivatives—which is certainly the case. But they could be more than that: they could radically alter the dynamics of equity investing ... The possibilities are huge, but as yet only dimly perceived.*
>
> David Lascelles in his report for the Centre for the Study of Financial Innovation, entitled *Single Stock Futures—The Ultimate Derivative?*

Exchanges

A non-exhaustive list of some of the major exchanges:

ADEX	Athens Derivatives Exchange
AMEX	American Stock Exchange
ASX	Australian Stock Exchange
BOE	Boston Options Exchange
Borsa Italiana	Italian Exchange
BSE	Boston Stock Exchange
BVLP	Portuguese Exchange
CBOE	Chicago Board Options Exchange
CBOT	Chicago Board of Trade
CME	Chicago Mercantile Exchange
EUREX	Swiss/German Derivatives Exchange
Euronext LIFFE	London International Financial Futures Exchange
HKEx	Hong Kong Exchanges and Clearing Limited
HSE	Helsinki Stock Exchange
IFE	Island Futures Exchange
ISE	International Securities Exchange
ISE	Irish Stock Exchange
JSE	JSE Securities Exchange South Africa
KCBOT	Kansas City Board of Trade
LSE	London Stock Exchange
MATIF	Marché à Terme International de France
ME	Bourse de Montreal (Montreal Exchange)
MEFF	Mercado Español de Futuros Financieros
NASDAQ	National Association of Securities Dealers Automatic Quotation System
NASDAQ LIFFE (NQLX)	Market for Single Stock Futures

NSE	National Stock Exchange (India)
NYMEX	New York Mercantile Exchange
NYSE	New York Stock Exchange
OneChicago	Chicago exchange combining CBT, CME, CBOE
PCE	Pacific Coast Exchange (San Francisco)
PE	Pacific Exchange
PHLX	Philadelphia Stock Exchange
SFE	Sydney Futures Exchange
SGX	Singapore Exchange Limited

Web acknowledgments

We would like to acknowledge the following institutions and their websites from which we were able to glean a significant amount of information, much of which contributed to the writing of this book:

Euronext.liffe	http://www.liffe.com
NQLX	http://www.nqlx.com
CFTC	http://www.cftc.gov
SFE	http://www.sfe.com.au
OneChicago	http://www.onechicago.com
SGX	http://www.sgx.com
ADEX	http://www.adex.ase.gr
STOXX	http://www.stoxx.com
MSCI	http://www.msci.com
Dow Jones Indexes	http://www.djindexes.com
MEFF	http://www.meff.es
erivatives.com	http://www.erivatives.com
SEC	http://www.sec.gov
NFA	http://www.nfa.futures.org
SIA	http://www.sia.com
NSE	http://www.nse-india.com
OCC	http://www.optionsclearing.com
ISE	http://www.iseoptions.com
CBOE	http://www.cboe.com
DTCC	http://www.dtcc.com
PHLX	http://www.phlx.com
NYSE	http://www.nyse.com
CSFI	http://www.csfi.org.uk

Bibliography

Beddis, Mark (2002) *SSFs—A Product in Search of a Market*. Online at: http://www.appliederivatives.com

Carret, Philip L. (1997) *The Art of Speculation*, John Wiley & Sons (ISBN 0-471-18187-9).

Fridson, Martin (ed.), Mackay, Charles and de la Vega, Joseph (1996) *Extraordinary Popular Delusions and the Madness of Crowds and Confusión de Confusiones*, John Wiley & Sons (ISBN 0-471-13312-4).

Garnick, Diane (2002) Quoted in "Security futures: The buy side speaks out." *Futures Industry Magazine*, September/October.

Greenberg, Steven A. (2002) *Single Stock Futures: The Complete Guide*, Traders Press Inc. (ISBN 0-934380-78-3).

Gupta, L.C. (2002) *Short Selling and Its Regulation in India: An International Perspective*, NSE Research Initiative Paper No. 2, National Stock Exchange of India Limited.

Kindleberger, Charles P. (1993) *A Financial History of Western Europe*, Oxford University Press (ISBN 0-19-507737-7).

Moles, Peter and Terry, Nicholas, (1999) *The Handbook of International Financial Terms*, Oxford University Press (ISBN 0-19-829481-6).

Rothchild, John (1998) *The Bear Book—Survive and Profit in Ferocious Markets*, John Wiley & Sons (ISBN 0-471-19718-1).

Rzepczynski, Mark (2002) Quoted in "Security futures: The buy side speaks out." *Futures Industry Magazine*, September/October.

Schultz, Harry D. (2002) *Bear Market Investing Strategies*, John Wiley & Sons (ISBN 0-470-84702-6).

Sutcliffe, Charles M.S. (1993) *Stock Index Futures: Theories and International Evidence*, Chapman & Hall (ISBN 0-412-40940-2).

Young, Patrick (2003) *New Capital Market Revolution: The Winners, Losers and the Future of Finance*, Texere Publishing (ISBN 1-587-99146-2).

Index